School governo

Third edition

A Handbook of guidance for governors of
county and voluntary schools

Written by
Keith Anderson, David Cook and Tony Saunders
on behalf of the
Society of Education Officers

LONGMAN
London and New York

SCHOOL GOVERNORS THIRD EDITION

Published by Longman Industry and Public Service Management, Longman Group UK Ltd, Westgate House, The High, Harlow, Essex CM20 1YR, UK.
Telephone: (0279) 442601
Fax: (0279) 444501

First published 1992

A catalogue record for this book is available from the British Library

ISBN 0–582–08808–9

Printed in Malaysia by PA

Contents

Foreword

In June 1991, the Society of Education Officers published *'Organisation of Local Government: The Future of the Education Service'*. At the beginning of this publication the Society states:

> Roles and responsibilities within the nationally maintained education system have changed radically in recent years. Many of these changes have been welcomed by the Society. Indeed, education officers have been the driving force behind the introduction of local management of schools and colleges, and the rapid devolution of resources and decision making to governing bodies.

It is, therefore, timely to publish the third edition of *'School governors'*. The Society recognises the need governors have, in the light of their devolved responsibilities, for clear, well informed guidance on their management obligations, and has responded as part of its support service commitment wherever that support is required. As a result of the tremendous amount of legislative change that has taken place within the education system, particularly following the 1988 Education Reform Act, and the increased responsibilities being given to governors, especially through financial delegation, this third edition is probably the most significant of the three. How much more pertinent today is the statement made by W. H. Petty, President, Society of Education Officers, 1980–81, in the foreword to the book's first edition:

> . . . the government of individual schools is particularly complex in our system.

As is the statement made by J. Beale, President, 1986–87, in the foreword to the book's second edition:

> Few will dispute that the recent pace of social and political change underlines the need for further detailed evaluation of the constitution, conduct and status of school governing bodies.

This book should do much to strengthen the already sound, constructive links between governors and education officers so that the education system managed locally may flourish in the interests of the young people of our country.

In commending this book most highly, I pay tribute to Ken

Brooksbank who was the person principally responsible for the first two editions and who died last year. A special word of thanks to Keith Anderson, Vice President of the Society, and colleagues David Cook and Tony Saunders for their work on this third edition.

As President, I am proud that in my year of office, the Society, through the leadership of its members, has been to the fore in ensuring that sound professional support is available to governors of schools at this most crucial period in educational history.

Tom Nolan, OBE, BA, MSSc, DipEd, FRSA
President of the Society of Education Officers 1991–92
Chief Executive
South Eastern Education and Library Board
Northern Ireland

1
Introduction

The realisation of an effective system of school governors has been slow. The requirement that each maintained school should have its own governing body was enacted in the Education Act of 1902 and has been repeated in every major Education Act since that date, but not until 1985 was the practice officially ended whereby local education authorities could group large numbers of schools under one governing body. It was the Taylor Report ('*A New Partnership for our Schools*') in June 1977 which triggered a renewed discussion of the nature and function of school governors. That discussion has been lively and widespread. The immediate result was the Education Act of 1980. Few measures have reflected a greater consensus of opinion than the clauses relating to school governors in that Act. The smooth development, which was confidently expected to follow, of a system of governing bodies acting as the guardians of the welfare, standards and standing of the school, did not occur. In some areas no change occurred; in others change was used to reinforce the control by one partner within the governing body, and many remained bodies without substance or clear identity and function.

Articles of government did not, generally speaking, do much to resolve the areas of overlap in the responsibilities of various bodies (government, local education authorities, governors, head teachers) involved in the provision and conduct of the school. The historic position where the functions of governors were prescribed by the local education authority continued, resulting in a wide diversity of practice. In a very short time after the 1980 Act, which was acclaimed as introducing a powerful system of school government, many were openly asking, 'Are school governors important?' and being very doubtful as to the answer.

Impact of change

Trends which were strongly discernible in 1980, such as the awareness of individual rights and freedoms, the acknowledgement of a more substantial role for parents and the maturity of older pupils, had been accentuated and accompanied by great social changes. Events have — often violently — forced attention on the fundamental fabric of our society. The place and attitudes of 'minorities' have changed, bringing a greater critical awareness of standards, relationships and 'the quality of society' — issues reflected powerfully in education and the schools. Families and parents are again being looked to as the prime instruments for ensuring social stability and cohesion.

At the same time the schools are held responsible for their part — or failure — in educating young people to produce a peaceful, stable, skilled, healthy, caring, enterprising and moral society. The economic affairs of the nation place a premium on industrial productive efficiency and increasingly schools are being assessed by quasi industrial criteria. Thus, terms such as cost effectiveness, value for money, quality and output are frequently applied to schools where efficient management, accountability, assessment and tendering for resources are being demanded. Those staffing the schools have naturally not remained unaffected by the advent of industrial or commercial attitudes to education. Yet what parents want is simply a good school for their children, and it is the responsibility of the governors to exercise their functions to provide a good school.

Recent research has shown that one of the major hindrances to effective work by governing bodies has been their uncertainty of purpose, while the courts have clearly affirmed the inescapable duty of governors to govern. By attempting to clarify issues which had hitherto obscured governors' powers and functions, the 1986 Education Act aimed to help resolve this dilemma. However scarcely was the ink on that legislation dry when it became clear that major new legislation was on the way. It appeared in 1988 as the Education Reform Act which has been described with some justification as the most significant piece of educational legislation since the 1944 Act. The catalogue of organisational and operational change it has brought about is well known. It includes a National Curriculum, greater parental choice over school admissions, schemes of financial delegation to governing bodies and the establishment of grant maintained schools and city technology colleges.

The 1988 Education Reform Act brings into the open a further agenda, and one which is confirmed in more recent government proposals. It is that the role of local education authorities is intended to be changed significantly, in simplest terms from being provider to enabler. This is not the place to discuss the reasons for such changes or their justification but what is clear is that governing bodies will be expected to become more accountable and responsible alongside their increased freedom and discretion.

Society is changing and the pace of change is accelerating. Consensus as to the nature of the education system that society requires and of the aims of education grows more remote in the ferment of change. In consequence the task of educational policy makers, whether at local, regional or national level, becomes more difficult in reconciling increased expectations with diminished resources, and fundamental values with skills for the changing future. Both local government and central government are forced into a situation where short-term policy predominates over long range strategy. Governors have therefore a very difficult assignment in working within the framework of local and central educational policy which is, particularly at the moment, uncertain and often ill-defined. It does mean however that governors have a constant need to inform themselves and to be informed if they are to operate effectively.

Despite the trend towards greater independence for individual schools the pressures from outside are such that it becomes increasingly difficult for any school, however large, to be self-contained. Shortage of specialist staff, vocationally orientated education initiatives, the economic provision of advanced studies, the need to operate economically and take advantage of scale of resources — these are a few of the reasons which make it imperative that schools should co-operate with each other, with colleges of further education, and industry and with their local communities. An efficient governing body must therefore not only understand its own school thoroughly, but must also be aware of how other institutions can complement the educational opportunities afforded by the school.

Factually, governors should know where to turn for the support which agencies outside the school can offer.

Aim of the book

Local education authorities are required to secure such training for governors as they think requisite. Whether the training is provided directly by the local education authority or through an agent such as a university, it is to be expected that governors will be supplied with or have access to certain basic documents. These may include the articles of government for the school, any explanatory book of guidance for governors produced by the authority, public statutory statements about its policy issued by the authority, and regulations and guidance relating to the management of the school's budget.

The aim of this book is neither to supersede nor to duplicate these documents. It seeks in a concise and easily accessible frame of reference to help governors to a clearer understanding of their role and function, and of the intricate context and complexities of relationships within which that function is to be exercised. It is hoped that the book will prove a useful supplement to the training offered by local education authorities and that it will be of value to elected members, governors, head teachers and managers in helping to promote a truly effective system of school government.

Two essential points remain to be made. First, it has been assumed that governors are carrying responsibility for a school with a delegated budget in the terms of the 1988 Education Reform Act. Secondly, for the sake of brevity and consistency the masculine form of pronouns and adjectives has been used throughout. Anyone familiar with schools and their governance will understand that this is simply a linguistic convention, and one which belies the prominent role of women in all aspects of school life.

2
The place of governing bodies in the education system

One of the outcomes of the 1988 Education Reform Act was a major shift in the traditional balance of power and influence between the partners in the education system. New duties and responsibilities were given to governing bodies, the Secretary of State acquired a significant number of new powers, and the role of the LEA was changed fundamentally. That change has continued as responsibility for higher education has passed away from LEAs, and Training and Enterprise Councils have begun to play an increasingly important role in the provision of training and education/industry links. In the White Paper 'Education and Training for the 21st Century' (1991), Government declared its intention to remove further education and sixth form colleges from local authority control. The proposed review of the structure and internal management of local authorities could well result in even more change.

This chapter simply sets out in brief outline the duties and responsibilities of those involved in the education system of the country as they currently exist.

Contributors to the educational system

The four principal contributors to the system may be identified as:

Central government
Local education authorities
Governing bodies
Head teachers and school staffs.

Parents have a legal duty to ensure that their children receive efficient full-time education suitable to their age, ability and aptitude either by regular attendance at school or otherwise. Equally, the Secretary of State and local education authorities must have regard to the fact that, as far as is practicable, children should be educated in accordance with the wishes of their parents. Much greater emphasis was given to the parental role by the 1986 Education Act and that role as part of the system is amplified in later chapters. The direct legal responsibility of the parent relates to the education of the individual child: that is, the total development of the child, mental, moral, physical, social and spiritual.

1. **Central government.** Through Acts of Parliament and Orders made under those Acts, central government determines the nature, scope and limitations of the educational system and prescribes who shall have specific responsibilities for the operation of the system, e.g. the Secretary of State for Education and Science, local education authorities, voluntary bodies (churches etc.) school governors, head teachers and parents.

    Central Government controls the overall levels of public expenditure, allocates general and specific grants, and monitors educational spending.

    Central government departments
    (a) Department of Education and Science
           Secretary of State for Education and Science
    (b) Welsh Office
           Secretary of State for Wales

    The Welsh Office is empowered to exercise functions in respect of primary and secondary education in Wales.

    Duty of the Secretary of State for Education and Science. Education Act 1944 Section 1.

    > It shall be the duty of the Secretary of State for Education and Science to promote the education of the people of England and Wales and the progressive development of institutions devoted to that purpose, and to secure the effective execution by local authorities under this control and direction of the national policy for providing a varied and comprehensive service in every area.

    The principal responsibilities of the Secretaries of State include:

    — establishing and keeping under review a National Curriculum;
    — approval of the provision and closure of schools;

- approval of the character of schools, e.g. grammar, grant maintained, 11–18;
- determining the standards for school buildings;
- approval of schemes for local management of schools and colleges;
- providing for initial teacher training;
- providing for the inspection of schools;
- securing that local education authorities provide a varied and comprehensive system of education in their area;
- ensuring the reasonable exercise of functions by local education authorities.

In particular, the Secretary of State is the final point of appeal within the system on many issues, e.g., appeals against the statement of special educational needs, refusal to meet parental choice of school, a dispute between the LEA and a governing body, or complaints that the local authority is acting unreasonably.

2. **Local education authorities.** Following the abolition of the Inner London Education Authority in 1990, the local education authorities of England and Wales are:

47 county councils (eight in Wales)
36 metropolitan district councils
20 Outer London borough councils
13 Inner London borough councils (including City of London Council)

Duty of the local education authority:
Within its area the duty of the Local Education Authority is to put into effect the national policy for providing a varied and comprehensive education, and, where necessary, to collaborate with other local education authorities to do so.

Amongst the principal responsibilities of the local education authority are:

- to provide schools sufficient in number, character and equipment to give all children in their area varied educational opportunities suitable to their age, ability and aptitude;
- to determine the place of schools in the educational system in their area;
- to ensure the National Curriculum is implemented;
- to establish schemes for the local financial management of schools;

— to inspect schools and ensure the implementation of the National Curriculum;
— to make provision for children with special educational needs;
— to secure the provision of appropriate ancillary and welfare services;
— to provide a careers service;
— to exercise its discretion to make grants to students.

The local education authority, in its broad capacity of supporting the implementation of national policy, is accountable through its wide range of functions to the Secretary of State for Education and Science and to the community which it serves for the reasonable, economic provision of education of quality and relevance over the whole spectrum of educational concern.

3. **Governing bodies.** Legally, governing bodies are required for:

county primary and secondary schools
voluntary primary and secondary schools
special schools
grant maintained schools
establishments of further education.

Duty of governing bodies:
Within the framework of national educational policy and of the policies and rules of the local education authority, the duty of governing bodies is to exercise the powers detailed in the articles of government to support the efficient conduct, development and welfare of the individual schools. Governors of voluntary schools will also have regard to the provisions of the trust deed in performing their duties.

In the exercise of their duties, governors of schools are to be accountable:

(i) to the Secretary of State for Education and Science who may require reports, returns and information from governors;
(ii) to the local education authority which may require reports from the governing body and has power to take steps which may be necessary to prevent the breakdown of discipline or to ensure effective financial management in the school;
(iii) to the parents to whom the governing body is required to present an annual report to be discussed at the annual parents' meeting.

More detailed information about governors' responsibilities is given in later chapters.

4. **The head teacher.** It is required by law that in every school there shall be a head teacher.

The school is the point at which the responsibilities of all the partners — central government, local education authorities, governing bodies, parents, trustees, and teachers coincide and are embodied in a detailed programme to deliver an education appropriate to each individual child.

Principal responsibilites of the head teacher:
(i)   the conduct and curriculum of the school
(ii) discipline
(iii) staff development.

Two further points are worth making about the system:

(a) The functions of the four major contributors vary in scope (the Secretary of State's responsibilities are for England and Wales, the governors' responsibilities are for a single school), but all the elements of the system exist principally to secure educational opportunity and development for each individual pupil.

(b) The contributors are each dependent on the other. It is futile for central and local government to provide buildings, money and other resources if the teachers in the classroom are ineffective. Equally, the most skilled teacher cannot be effective without proper support from governors, local education authorities and central government.

These points are simply, perhaps over-simply, expressed because it is vital that they should be understood if governors are to have a proper appreciation of their function.

Constitution of governing bodies

The 1986 Education Act provided that the constitution of governing bodies of county, voluntary and special schools maintained by a local education authority should be determined by an instrument of government made by order of the local education authority. Such instruments must conform to the conditions laid down in the Act and the local education authority is required to consult the governing body before making the order.

In the case of voluntary schools, the local education authority must secure the agreement of the governing body to the order. Where an instrument of government is embodied or varied by the order, the agreement of the foundation governors is required and they may propose alterations on matters of particular concern to them. In the event of failure to reach agreement or to accept alterations proposed by foundation governors, the local authority or the governors may refer the matter to the Secretary of State who shall direct as he thinks fit (including, if necessary, modification of the trust deed).

The instrument of government must contain provisions required by the 1986 Education Act or any other enactment. This means that the size and the constituent elements of the governing body are determined by law. In practice it may well be that governors exercise their functions so that the category of each is not seen to be material, but it is important that the rationale underlying the legal requirement should be understood. In county and controlled schools, the local education authority, teachers, parents, foundation governors and co-opted governors make up the governing body in such a way that no one category has an automatic constitutional majority. In aided or special agreement schools, there are no co-opted governors, but, constitutionally, foundation governors must outnumber the other governors.

There are then two occasions on which governors will be concerned with their own constitution:

(a) initially when the local education authority is drawing up the instrument of government;
(b) whenever co-opted governors are to be appointed.

Co-opted governors may be selected individuals or designated office-holders (the vicar for instance) deemed suitable to enhance the governors' exercise of functions. In particular, the connection between the governing body and the local business community must be taken into account by governors in making co-options. The knowledge and judgement of the governors is of paramount importance here.

The precise constitutions of governing bodies which must be included in instruments of government are detailed in Sections 3 and 4 of the 1986 Act, and are summarised here in appendix B.

Duration/Termination of appointment

All governors of county, controlled and special schools, except the head, are appointed for a period of four years. They may stand for re-election at the end of that period, subject to continuing eligibility within the appropriate category.

> *Parent governors* do not have to stand down if their child leaves the school during their period of office, though they may do so if they wish.
> *Representative governors* can be removed by the body (LEA or Minor Authority) which appointed them.
> *Teacher governors* must stand down from the governing body when they leave the school.
> *Co-opted governors* are chosen by the other governors. They cannot be removed from office by those who selected them.
> *Foundation governors* can be removed from office at any time by the people who appointed them.

Grouping of schools

The local education authority may group two or more schools under a single governing body constituted under a single instrument of government:

(i) *Without the consent of the Secretary of State.*
If the group consists only of two primary schools which serve substantially the same area.

Before resolving to group two primary schools the local education authority must consult the governing bodies concerned, and in the event of a dispute as to whether the two schools are to be regarded as serving the same area, the Secretary of State shall determine.

In Wales there is a further qualification that there must be no significant difference between the two schools in their use of the Welsh language.

(ii) *With the consent of the Secretary of State.*
The group may include county, aided, controlled or maintained special schools. The single governing body will then have the constitution of an aided school if there is an aided school in the group, of a controlled school if there is a controlled school but no aided school in the group, or of a maintained special school if there is a special school but no controlled or aided school in the group. Only if all the schools are county schools will the governing body be that of a county school.

Before taking any resolution which affects an existing school the local authority must first consult the governing body.

In giving consent to a proposal to group schools the Secretary of State may impose limits as to the duration of the grouping to which his consent is given, and may by order bring to an end any grouping of schools for which his consent was required at any time.

Such proposals may not arise frequently. Where they do, governors will need to be aware of the nature of all schools in the group, and must exercise careful judgement in the context of their local knowledge in reacting to consultation on issues which may be complex since they affect several schools and their immediate communities.

Election of parent governors

In a county, controlled or maintained special school, the local education authority must make all the arrangements for the election of parent governors by secret ballot, although they may delegate some of the work. In aided schools the governors have this responsibility.

The arrangements must include informing parents of the vacancy, of their right to stand as a candidate and to vote, and arranging for parents to vote.

Wherever possible, vacancies among parent governors are to be filled by election. However, there are two sets of circumstances in which it might not be possible for parent governors to be elected. These are:

— if at any school there are fewer parents standing for election than vacancies to be filled;
— if at a boarding school where more than half the pupils are boarders, the LEA decides it would not be practicable to hold an election, and the instrument of government allows for the possibility of filling vacancies by appointment.

In these cases, any vacancies may be filled by someone chosen by the other members of the governing body. They should seek to appoint someone who is a parent of a pupil at the school or someone who has children of school age. They must not appoint in these circumstances an elected member or an employee of the LEA, an employee of any voluntary aided school which the LEA maintains, or a co-opted member of any of the LEA's education committees. (There is, however, no bar on anyone in these categories standing for election as a parent governor.)

Questions and answers.

Some queries about governor categories

Q. *Can a member of the teaching staff who is also a parent of a child who is in the school seek election as a parent governor?*

A. He may, provided that he is not elected as a teacher governor.

Q. *Can the head teacher who has a child in the school be elected as a parent governor?*

A. No. The head teacher is entitled to be a governor by virtue of office. If he chooses not to be a governor as head, he revokes his right to be a governor and consequently cannot be elected in any other capacity.

Q. *What is the position of a councillor who is a member of the education committee but is not appointed as a governor by the local education authority? Can he be a parent governor or co-opted to the governing body?*

A. Yes, although it should be noted that the governors are prohibited from appointing such a person as a parent governor where (in a boarding school, for example) the governors have the right to appoint. In co-opting members, governors will no doubt remember that one of the objectives of the 1986 legislation was to avoid a majority by any one element of the governing body.

Q. *If two schools are grouped with one governing body, are the head teachers of both schools entitled to be governors?*

A. Yes, unless they choose not to be so.

Q. *Can a teacher who is also a parent be a candidate for the position of teacher and parent governor?*

A. Nobody can hold a governorship in two capacities. It is clearly wrong for a person to declare his intention of achieving an unlawful position and the teacher should therefore commit himself to candidature for one position only.

However, nobody is disqualified for election or appointment in one category of governor because he is qualified for election or appointment in another category (except the head teacher — see above).

Q. *How many governorships may a person hold at any one time?*

A. Following amendments to the 1989 Regulations, no person may hold more than two governorships at any time.

Some queries about grouping of schools

Q. *If schools are grouped how is the size of the single governing body determined?*

A. The sum of pupils on the registers of all the schools included in the group determines the size of the governing body.

Q. *What is the procedure for the election of parent governors?*

A. The procedure for the election of parent and teacher governors will be determined by the instrument of government which must ensure that there is no school within the group which will not have participated in the election of at least one of the parent or teacher governors. The procedure should be acceptable to all the schools since the local education authority is required to secure the agreement of the governors and of the foundation governors of each individual school in the proposed grouping before making the order embodying the instrument of government for the grouped schools.

Q. *Will it be entirely at the discretion of the governors to use any money for which they are given responsibility within the group?*

A. The powers of governors with regard to finance will be prescribed by the articles of government and the LMS policy rules of the authority which will most probably secure that the funds are spent on the individual school and will not be transferable in whole or in part to other schools within the group.

   Similarly, the private and trust funds for a voluntary school will be applicable to that school only, unless the trustees determine that they may be used in connection with a joint venture.

Q. *Will the information to be given to parents and others be issued separately for the individual schools or collectively for the group?*

A. Information must be given about each individual school but there would be no bar to the governors combining the information about individual schools in a common document for the group.

Q. *Will the schools in the group be required to adopt a common curriculum?*

A. Not totally. All schools are now required to follow the National Curriculum. Subject to that and the provisions of the 1988 Education Reform Act, each school's curriculum would be tailored to the ages and needs of the children within it.

Q. *Will the governors report to parents' meetings for each individual school?*
A. The 1986 Act empowers governors to hold a joint parents' meeting for all the schools within the group. If they do so, they may either prepare reports on the separate schools or a joint report which refers to matters of particular interest to each school separately within the report.

   If, at a joint parents' meeting, it is necessary to take a vote on a matter which affects some but not all of the schools in the group, only parents of registered pupils at the schools affected are allowed to vote.
Q. *What happens if one school in the group closes?*
A. If a school in the group closes, the local education authority must review the grouping and consider whether the grouping should continue. If the grouping required the approval of the Secretary of State, the authority must report to him the result of their review with such information as will enable him to decide whether the grouping should be brought to an end or not.
Q. *Can the grouping arrangement be brought to an end?*
A. If the group does not include a voluntary school, it can be brought to an end by resolution of the local education authority.

   If the group does include a voluntary school it may be brought to an end by:

(i) resolution of the authority made with the governors' agreement;
(ii) by one year's notice given by the authority to the governing body;
or
(iii) by one year's notice given by the governing body to the authority.

3
Practical aspects of governorship

The conduct of business by governing bodies is laid down in the Education Acts and in the School Government Regulations. Two crucial elements are:

1. **Frequency of meetings:** the governing body of the school must hold a meeting at least once in every term. Governors may hold meetings more frequently if there is business to be done and certainly the volume of business now before governors generally requires more than one meeting a term. Any three members of the governing body may requisition a meeting and it is the duty of the clerk to call such a meeting.

2. **Agenda:** the precise form of agenda will vary from one governing body to another. The agenda should, however, be drawn up and circulated to members to allow them ample time to read and understand the agenda before the meeting. Normally at least seven days' notice will be given but the chairman has power to reduce that time in cases of urgency.

   The agenda should be fully documented. Business not documented but merely reported orally or items tabled at the meeting are not conducive to considered and balanced decisions. Governors cannot be expected to fulfil their duties adequately in such circumstances. Equally, a governor who wishes to raise some matter at the governing body should give good notice so that the necessary preparations may be made to enable a full and informed debate to take place.

Three items may be expected to arise at each ordinary meeting of governors:

1. **Head teacher's report:** perhaps the most important item of business on any agenda will often be the head teacher's report. Surveys of educational effectiveness by

HMI have stressed the crucial nature of the leadership given by the head teacher. The style of leadership will vary enormously and so will the style of reporting by a head teacher to the governors. There can be no stereotype for what is essentially a personal interaction. However, there are some things which governors will expect to see in the head teacher's report:

(a) It should give them information about the school to enable them to carry out their functions, i.e. giving information to parents, establishing links with the local community, understanding the aims of the school and how those aims are being implemented.

(b) It should acquaint governors with significant change in such important areas as pupil numbers, building matters, curriculum considerations, school meals or transport. It should also consult governors on any significant changes which might be under consideration so that common policy might be agreed in advance of its introduction. The head's report is a vehicle by which governors become aware of growth and development within the school.

(c) It should also consider and evaluate the effect of actions or proposed actions of other bodies on the school, e.g. a proposal by the local education authority to amend its general policy on home–school transport.

(d) It should alert governors to the needs of the school and to its achievements.

(e) It should keep governors informed on the school's policy and performance in respect to children with special educational needs.

However well informed governors are about their school, the head teacher's report is an essential guide to the priorities and health of the establishment. It should never become a simple chronicle of school activities.

2. **Statement on the budget:** with the delegation of financial responsibility it is essential that the full governing body is kept informed about the state of the school budget and of any wider implications. Most schools will have established a finance sub-committee but the budget responsibility is for the full governing body to exercise.

3. **Policy documents circulated by the local education authority or the school:** it is essential that governors are kept informed of major policy developments within the school and within the local authority. A most valuable development has been the attendance at governing body meetings of members of the school or local education authority staff to speak on particular papers and to answer governors' questions.

Quorum

The quorum for the meeting of the governing body must be at least three members or, where greater, a third (rounded up to a whole number) of the total membership. The quorum becomes two-thirds when governors are exercising particular responsibilities — for example the co-option of governors or the appointment of sub-committees.

Absences

Provided that there is the necessary quorum of governors present, the conduct of business is not invalidated by the absence from the meeting of any member or by a vacancy in the total membership.

Right to attend meetings

Legally, only the head teacher and clerk have the absolute right to attend all governing body meetings. However, normal practice is to afford the right of attendance to the Chief Education Officer or his representative. It is for individual governing bodies to decide whether or not to admit the press and/or public, although either would have to be excluded for items of confidential business.

Voting

Decisions of the governing body are taken on a simple majority of governors present and voting, the chairman of the meeting having a casting vote in the event of a tie.

Governors will be required to withdraw from the meeting and not to vote in certain circumstances. Broadly speaking these are that the governor (or domestic partner) has a particular interest in a contract etc. under consideration, that he has a direct or personal interest in an appointment, or that he is personally involved in some disciplinary matter.

Minutes

The minutes of proceedings at meetings must be either entered in a book or entered on loose leaves consecutively numbered.

The minutes must be signed by the chairman at the next meeting and if the minutes are in loose leaf form every sheet must be initialled. This is a safeguard, arising from experience, against falsification of minutes and corruption.

The information which must be made available as soon as possible at the school is the agenda, the draft minutes (following approval by the chairman), the signed minutes and any reports or any papers considered at the meeting.

Minutes relating to an individual or to any matter deemed confidential by the governors shall not be available for inspection.

Panels and sub-committees

It is for the governing body to appoint at least three members to the selection panel which will recommend to the full governing body the appointments of head teacher or deputy head teacher. The selection of other staff can be delegated by the full governing body to one or more governors, the chairman of governors or the head teacher acting on behalf of the governing body.

The increased volume of business for governors has led to an increase in the number of sub-committees undertaking detailed work on behalf of the full governing body. In many schools it is now customary to establish a finance sub-committee, a personnel sub-committee and a building sub-committee to undertake day to day responsibility for these important duties. There are, however, very important functions which governors are not allowed to delegate to a sub-committee. These duties are specified in the School Government Regulations and include many of governors' statutory responsibilities. One of the key responsibilities which it is now not possible to delegate to a sub-committee is the appointment of head teachers and deputy head teachers where the recommendation from a selection panel must be considered by the full governing body.

Chairman and vice-chairman

At their first meeting in each school year the governors are to elect from their members a chairman and vice-chairman. Although the tenure of office is for one year only, the chairman and vice-chairman are eligible, if still members of the governing body, to be re-elected for further terms of office. A governor who is employed at the school is not eligible to become chairman of governors.

The chair of the governing body will be taken at meetings by the chairman or, in his absence, by the vice-chairman. If neither is present, the governors will elect one of their members to chair the meeting.

The chairman may resign his office and must relinquish it on ceasing to be a member of the governing body. Casual vacancies in the office of chairman or vice-chairman are filled by election at the next meeting of the governors.

The chairman has a special position. In addition to conducting the meetings of the governors, he is seen by the public and parents as the spokesman of the governors. He will be consulted by the local education authority, sometimes formally but also informally, and less experienced colleagues will look to him for guidance, advice and support. Usually a close understanding will develop between the chairman and the head teacher. A chairman can be a real source of support for a head, sharing with him the problems which the head faces and which cannot easily be discussed within the school. In certain cases legal procedures require that the chairman of governors shall be consulted or informed, e.g. in disciplinary cases. The chairman must, therefore, be capable of independent decision and of accepting personal responsibility. These are qualities which governors will need to take into account when making their election. The onerous responsibilities of chairmanship also deserve special support from the local education authority, especially in its training programme.

Decisions may be required between meetings of governors. If the chairman feels sufficiently confident that he can correctly anticipate the wishes of the governors, he will act on their behalf, and on his decision action will be taken. In particular, the chairman has the power to act where any delay would be likely to be seriously harmful to the interest of the school or to the interest of any pupils, parents or staff. The principle of collective responsibility requires that action taken by the chairman on behalf of the governors should be reported and endorsed at the next meeting.

If the chairman feels that he is not able to take personal action or that delay would not cause extreme prejudice, he should arrange for a special meeting of the governors to be called.

Tenure of office

The instrument of government for county, controlled and special schools will provide for every governor (other than *ex officio* governors) to hold office for a term of four years.

Teacher governors who cease to be employed at the school are disqualified from continuing to hold office as governors but parent governors can serve out their remaining period of office after their child has left the school. A representative governor may be removed by the body which appointed him.

Disqualifications from office

A governor who, without the consent of the governing body, has failed to attend all meetings over a six month period is to be disqualified as a governor of that school. This regulation reflects the need for all governors to shoulder the responsibilities of governorship, although the provision for possible re-election would allow for genuine absence to be accounted for.

A person is also disqualified from holding office if he has been adjudged bankrupt. The disqualification holds for a period of three years from his discharge from bankruptcy.

A governor who has been convicted of any offence and has had passed on him a sentence of imprisonment (either suspended or not) for a period of not less than three months without the option of a fine will be disqualified. A person so convicted within five years of his election or appointment shall also be disqualified.

Governors' annual report

The purpose of the annual report from the governors is to account to parents on their stewardship of the school during the year. The information which is required to be included in the report will be detailed in the articles of government, it provides an opportunity, however, to go beyond the legal minima to convey to parents the key issues of the year.

Clearly, it is essential that the report should carry the support of all governors and although the task of drafting can be delegated to a sub-group the final draft should be approved by the full governing body. The report will go to a very mixed but interested readership who will appreciate straightforward language, layout and length. Governors should be sensitive to the need to provide the report in languages other than English if that is a significant local consideration.

The annual report is considered at a meeting to which all parents are invited. The purpose of the meeting is to enable parents to discuss matters arising from the annual report and there is power for the meeting to pass formal resolutions, subject to a minimum attendance equal to at least 20% of the pupil roll. However, prudent governors and prudent education authorities will pay careful regard to representations from parents' meetings, whatever the attendance.

Levels of attendance at annual parents' meetings have been very variable — however, low numbers should not easily be ascribed to parental apathy since all will have had the chance to read the report and may feel little need to hear it discussed. On the other hand, schools which have followed a lively report with a lively meeting (the annual report need not be the sole subject) have found their efforts rewarded by a good attendance. In the great majority of schools, the annual meeting offers an opportunity to celebrate success and to reinforce the partnership of governors, staff and parents.

Governors' expenses

Under the 1986 Education Act, LEAs have the power (but not the duty) to draw up schemes for the payment of travelling and subsistence allowances to governors, provided that all categories of governor on the same school are treated equally.

Information and training for governors

It was not until the 1986 Education Act that local authorities came under a duty to provide training for governors, although most authorities had already anticipated the need and had established local programmes. The exact legal requirements are:

Every local education authority shall secure:

(a) that every governor of a county, voluntary or special school maintained by them is provided (free of charge) with:

(i) a copy of the instrument of government, and of the articles of government, for the school; and

(ii) such other information as they consider appropriate in connection with the discharge of his functions as a governor; and

(b) that there is made available to every such governor (free of charge) such training as the authority consider necessary for the effective discharge of those functions.

In order to implement these legal requirements, government has made governor training one of its specified priorities within the support grants scheme (now entitled Grants for Education and Support Training). It is a requirement since 1992 that 50% of these funds are to be delegated to some or all individual school governing bodies to buy in the training that they themselves feel is necessary.

No doubt under the new arrangements there will still be considerable use made of the programmes provided by the governor training co-ordinators of local education authorities. With the very rapid change in educational law and the acquisition by governors of more and more responsibilities, training programmes have become more specialist, for example in the field of financial management. Equally, authorities have begun to target their courses more effectively, developing specialist materials for different groups, for example chairmen of governors or newly appointed governors, or for individual governing bodies.

Local authorities have been assisted in their role as trainers by national organisations such as Action for Governors' Information and Training (AGIT) and the National Association of Governors and Managers who have themselves produced excellent material and have held many national and local conferences.

The reconstitution of governing bodies now places a particularly important duty on LEAs. Not only is it essential that sufficient numbers of governors should offer themselves for election or appointment, it is crucial that they receive high quality training to enable them quickly to become effective in their role.

It is evident that training for governors is not a one-off activity but must be built into a local education authority's system of on-going support. It is just as important to educational quality as is a sound and varied programme of teacher in-service training. As governors build up experience so they themselves will feed back information to improve the training programmes.

4
Getting to know the school

The responsibilities of a governing body are very considerable. Even though the head teacher is there to support the governors in the discharge of those responsibilities, the ultimate account- ability for some policies and actions rests with the governors and not the head. The general responsibility for the effective management of the school, for ensuring that the delegated budget is properly and effectively used, for staff appointments, dismissals and — to some extent — salaries, for pupil exclusions, for curriculum policy and for reporting to parents, means that a governor needs a very full understanding of the way in which the school operates if the discharge of those responsibilities is going to be effective and in the interest of all pupils. To know a school in some depth requires from a governor time and a willingness to learn and understand. Without such knowledge, governors will be limited in their effectiveness.

Practical steps

However much advance paperwork a new governor is given, the best way of getting to know the school is to visit when it is in operation. Normal governors' meetings do not afford this op- portunity, although they are a valuable training ground in giving new governors the chance to learn from more experienced colleagues. Even teacher governors, who would be expected to know the school as part of their professional commitment, might find there are aspects of the school and its government about which they, too, can have much to learn through carefully structured visits.

Governors are not school inspectors and do not have the same right of access to the school as an inspector. However, few head teachers would seek to deny or impede access to the school by governors. On the contrary head teachers, when approached, will welcome the interested governor and do everything possible to make a governor's visits interesting and productive. Teachers may normally be expected to welcome governors to their classrooms, provided that due warning of the visit has been given and that governors recognise that their learning about the school, important as it is, must not disrupt the fundamental business of the school, the education of the pupils. Most head teachers will help governors to conduct their visits, so that they derive benefit from seeing the school working normally. Some local education authorities produce guidelines to assist governors in school visiting.

Complementary to the school visit is the practice adopted in many schools of having a head of department or another teacher reporting to the governors at their meeting on some particular aspect of the school's work, for instance the school's method of teaching reading or the school's environmental education policy. A variant of this good practice, adopted by some governing bodies, is to ask a small group of members to familiarise themselves with some facet of the school's work and to report their findings to the rest of the governing body.

In a number of schools, particularly the larger ones, governors are 'attached' to individual departments, to form close links with the staff there and others through their deeper knowledge of a particular subject area, to gain a better perception of how the school as a whole operates, of its strengths and weaknesses, its concerns and aspirations. Most governing bodies have now established a number of sub-committees to consider in depth different aspects of the governors' functions, e.g. finance, curriculum strategies, special educational needs, pupil discipline, staff appointments, and to advise the full governing body as appropriate. An individual governor's contribution to the life of the school through such approaches can be very considerable.

The importance of the documents, (including the head teacher's report) which the school prepares on policy matters within the school, should not be underrated. Many schools circulate such documents to governors and the discussion of them which follows is a very valuable way of gaining knowledge of the working and aims of the school, particularly in the context of perceptions already acquired by visiting the school.

Questions and answers

Q. *What can a governor do if reasonable requests to visit the school are coldly received by the head teacher, who is clearly obstructive?*

A. A governor can raise the matter with the chairman, who may be able to resolve the position. If this is not effective, there is a breakdown of trust and confidence between the governors and the school. A governor (or the chairman) can then bring the matter before the governors to examine the causes of the breakdown (which are rarely only one-sided) and to find ways of remedying them.

Q. *How can I get to know the school when my work prevents me from visiting the school when it is in session?*

A. Apart from reading school documents and discussions with fellow governors, attendance at out-of-school functions is useful, but many head teachers are very willing to give time to governors to talk to them about the school when governors can manage to visit out-of-school times. Nonetheless, the real atmosphere of the school can be appreciated and fully understood only from first-hand experience of the work situation.

Q. *On visiting a school I find an atmosphere which is far from the harmonious, happy and purposeful one depicted by the head teacher in his report to the governors. What can I do?*

A. Although governors have a particular responsibility for the oversight of the curriculum, that is, what the school intends to teach, their responsibility extends also to those elements which are not directly academic. An unhappy school clearly has shortcomings. A governor's first action should be to check with the head teacher. There may be circumstances which are beyond the head's control and which have changed his otherwise accurate representation of the school, for example an industrial dispute which deeply divides and affects staff attitudes to their teaching, or a remark by a politician may have started rumours affecting the future viability of the school. If the head is not able to accept the governor's view, or alternatively to explain the situation, then the governor should check with colleagues to ensure that the view is not mistaken but shared by other governors. The chairman of the governors should then be asked to advise the head teacher of the governors' specific concerns with a view to having improvements made. Finally, the governing body may be alerted formally and an investigation set up to reveal circumstances, such as a head struggling against serious illness which is impairing his efficiency, a serious conflict between head and deputy which prevents either from seeing clearly the tensions created in the school, or a bigoted teacher whose advocacy of his own views is disrupting the staff, creating an unhappy state which the head believes that he can restore, given enough time. The governors may then need to consider the options open to them to resolve the difficulties.

Relations with the local community

Few pieces of legislation have commanded the widespread support which was accorded to the provisions of the 1980 Education Act relating to governing bodies. Nor did any of the regulations or measures included in the 1986 Education Act do anything to diminish that support. The individual school governing body — with augmented strength in parents and locally co-opted members — is seen to have an increasingly important place in the quest for 'quality' in the education service. Stress on the role of schools in producing people with the right qualifications and attitudes to deliver the country from its besetting problems has focused the anxieties of the community on the performance of the schools by which it is served.

The relationship of the school with the community is, in part, laid down in legislation. Every local education authority is required to publish specific information about individual schools, including information about the school curriculum and examination policy and performance. It must include the name, address and telephone number of the chairman of governors who must be clearly accessible to any member of the community. Each individual governor has to be named in the governors' annual report to parents, in which the governors are required to account for the discharge of their functions. The parents' meeting is open not only to parents of children in the school but also to such other persons as the governing body may invite. In practice, governors may have difficulty in refusing to invite any person who wishes to attend. Inescapably, therefore, governors have a close relationship with the community served by the school, which has the right to discuss governors' actions.

In making co-options to the governing body, governors must have regard to the extent to which governors are members of the local business community and, if necessary, use the co-options to increase those links.

On matters relating directly to the school, most people will find that the head teacher is the first person to whom they will turn, but some may well find it easier to approach a lay governor. A parent who thinks that a teacher has acted unfairly toward his child may well feel that unbiased information on school discipline cannot be obtained from the head teacher and will therefore turn to the governors. They may tender the same advice as the head teacher, but the parent may find that advice from a layman's viewpoint is very reassuring.

Many local authorities have a deliberate policy of using schools for community purposes. In small rural schools there is often a very close identity between the school, the governors and the community, with the school acting as the community centre. Hence, many proposed closures of rural schools have been opposed, on the grounds that they would deprive the community of its social centre.

This interaction between school and community which arises naturally in some rural settings is manifest in much larger and less well-defined communities. Instances are on record where public or community were so concerned that a prescribed book in a public examination was contrary to the ethical standards expected in the school that they recommended — and secured — its withdrawal. There was a case of the public objecting to allegedly unacceptable bias in the teaching of history in a school, causing an inquiry to be held and modifications in the teaching to be introduced.

The 1986 Education Act provides that where political issues are brought to the attention of pupils either at school or in activities organised by or on behalf of the school, governors and the head must take steps to ensure that pupils are offered a balanced presentation of opposing views. On the other hand, schools have contributed, through involvement of parents in the school, and by providing parents' rooms in the school, where adult group activities have developed, to the generation of activity and confidence which has had a healthy regenerative influence on the community serving the school. These are striking examples of the process of interaction between school and community which is occurring, though generally perhaps less dramatically. Governors have the vital role of catalysts or intermediaries. At least one authority takes such a serious view of this role as to suggest that governors should live within the catchment area of the school.

Governors have a responsibility for the control of and the use of the premises out of school hours. Some applications for use of the school premises may be prejudicial to the good conduct of the school and governors will have the duty of deciding to refuse a request from a section of the community in the interests of the school. On the other hand, some lettings would be offensive to the community on moral, racial or political grounds and the governors have to have regard to the prevailing views of the community in exercising their control. These issues are also addressed in chapter 12.

Interest in community education and in the development of community schools is growing. Local authorities are adding facilities to schools for community use; for example, with the help of the Sports Council, squash courts have been built on to primary schools. Schools have been designed so that their buildings can be used by the public; for instance, swimming baths, gymnasia, school meals facilities. Parents and others are involved in the school, sometime as students, and there are instances when pre-school provision is made in the school to help parents to participate in activities and to afford senior pupils opportunities for practical experience in connection with their school courses. At this interface between school and community governors' functions are called into play; for example, overseeing the curriculum, conduct of the school and the use of premises and resources.

A different interpretation of the governors' role occurs when the local education authority has deliberately designed the school as an integral part of a community complex.

For example, part of the school may be built over a shopping complex, the public library and the school library are joined in the same building, the swimming bath and gymnasium are designed for joint adult/school use, the school playing field is the local athletics stadium, the school hall shares a stage with the community theatre, and meals provision is integrated with catering for the public. Not only is accommodation jointly available, but the times of availability overlap. The school is inextricably of the community and the community is inevitably aware of and involved in the school. The role of governors in such circumstances becomes more complex; for instance, where there is use and maintenance of equipment which may be purchased by the school or the community but is available to both, such as visual aids, stage equipment or computers. Sometimes the governors are completely responsible — this is normally the case for example in primary schools — but sometimes they will share their responsibilities with others in managing the community provision or complex. The precise functions will vary, but they will certainly involve governors in close relations with the community.

Governors will expect to have relations with the community

through their co-opted members who, though in no sense delegates, may be expected to represent the background from which they are appointed, for example the local business community, industry, commerce and the Church.

Last, but by no means least, are the links that each school should make with other educational establishments in the locality; a secondary school with its contributory primary schools, a school or college with the local youth club, a primary school with the pre-school playgroup, and a number of small primary schools with each other. In this way skills and resources are shared to mutual benefit, and educational development is seen as a progression for each individual school.

5
Admission of pupils

It has long been a principle that pupils should be educated in accordance with the wishes of their parents, provided this is compatible with good education and a reasonable use of public funds. The 1980 Education Act gave much greater practical effect to this principle, and parents are now entitled, with the help of published information, to express preferences as to which schools they wish their children to attend. Those preferences then have to be met except in certain narrowly defined circumstances. Under the more open enrolment provisions of the 1988 Education Reform Act, admission levels cannot be set below the standard number for admissions. This standard number is ultimately related to the physical capacity of the school rather than to any artificial planning level.

Parental wishes

The arrangements for admissions to county schools are generally made by the local education authority, which is responsible for the size of the school, its character (in the technical sense of status, e.g. comprehensive or grammar) and its place in the educational system. Unless otherwise provided for in the articles of government, the governors will have little direct responsibility for admissions, but they have the right to be consulted over the general arrangements and to comment on them as they affect their school. In voluntary aided schools, the governors are responsible for admissions but they must act in accordance with arrangements agreed with the local authority.

All arrangements must embrace a proper recognition of both the principle and practice of parental preference. In Section 76 of the 1944 Act:

> . . . local education authorities shall have regard to the general principle that, so far as is compatible with the provision of efficient instruction and training, and the avoidance of unreasonable public expenditure, pupils are to be educated in accordance with the wishes of their parents.

Furthermore 'a pupil shall not be refused admission to or excluded from a school on other than reasonable grounds'.

That principle is made even more explicit in the 1980 Education Act and the 1988 Education Reform Act brought in further measures to remove what were seen as remaining barriers to the achievement of parental preference.

Parental preference in practice

Under the 1980 Education Act, the LEA must make arrangements to enable the parents of children who are in their area to express a preference as to the school they wish their children to attend, and to give reasons for that preference. A duty is laid upon the local education authority, and on the governors of a county or voluntary school, to comply with parental preferences expressed in accordance with the authority's arrangements, except where this would:

(a) prejudice the provision of efficient education or the efficient use of resources;
(b) for an aided or special agreement school, be incompatible with the arrangements for the admission of pupils to the school agreed between the school governors and the local education authority;
(c) for a school whose admission arrangements are based wholly or partly on selection by reference to ability or aptitude, be incompatible with selection under those arrangements.

The definition of 'efficient education' and 'efficient use of resources' can be a matter of fine judgement in a complex situation. Authorities try to ensure that children of all abilities have access to the widest possible range of educational, social and extra-curricular opportunities relevant to their own needs that can be provided within the resources available. Those objectives may not be satisfactorily met if, for example, some teaching groups become over-large and schools over-crowded or, conversely, if pupil numbers in other schools decline so far that peer groups of reasonable size and compatibility can no longer be established, and the staffing and physical resources allocated to the school are markedly less than can be provided for other similar pupils in the locality. The authority's plans must, therefore, take into account the needs of all the children in the area, and the effect of a fair and effective distribution of the resources available.

Standard numbers

The government felt some concern that such planning mechanisms might prevent the fullest possible achievement of parental preferences. For example, under the 1980 Education Act a planned admission level (PAL) might be set to limit the intake to an oversubscribed school while places were offered at an alternative and undersubscribed school.

In the 1988 Education Reform Act, the government included provisions for more open enrolment (MOE) and the replacement of the planned admission levels of the 1980 Act by the new concept of the standard number for admissions (SNA).

The standard number has applied to secondary school admissions since September 1990, and to primary schools from September 1992. It is defined as the highest of a series of historical peaks in the school's admissions but ultimately must relate to the school's physical capacity. In Circular 11/88 the DES makes it clear that the intention is that applicants will not be denied admission until schools are physically full. A method for assessing the physical capacity of schools is provided for local authorities and governors.

Publication of admission arrangements

The information that LEAs, and the governors of aided schools, are required to publish over admission arrangements must include the number of pupils it is planned to admit in any year, and the criteria which will be applied for determining priorities between applications if places at a particular school are oversubscribed. These arrangements will vary from one authority to another but may take into account such factors as an older brother or sister attending the preferred school, medical reasons, geographical proximity as well as the length and complexity of the journey from home, single sex and co-educational options and elements of specific curriculum choice (e.g. opportunities for pupils with particular interests or talents to study minority subjects such as music, second and third languages or particular sporting opportunities). It will readily be appreciated that although consideration of these factors is generally accepted, the details can give rise to considerable dispute with parents who are trying to make the strongest case for their child.

In the case of voluntary aided and special agreement schools it is essential that admission arrangements are clearly and specifically agreed between the school governors and the local education authority and appropriately published.

Where selective arrangements apply, the process of selection should be clearly explained and governors should be aware of the procedures. It is important to note that in a grammar school where admission is based on selection there is no requirement to admit up to the standard number if there are insufficient candidates meeting the required level of ability.

Governors of both county and voluntary schools will need to have an awareness of the relevant criteria for admissions, and how they affect their school. Some schools still feel they have their own 'catchment' areas. While the concept of a catchment area has less relevance since the 1980 Act, many authorities still try to identify designated admission areas for particular schools in order to simplify the process of admissions and to give parents some security of expectation over, for example, admission to their neighbouring school. Parents who live outside the designated admission area of a school (or even its maintaining LEA) have the right to express a preference for that school, and their claims must be properly considered under the admissions criteria. Governors have an important advisory role to play here, keeping the authority informed and updated on changes and developments in the links between the local community and the school. Under the 1986 Education Act, the LEA and governors are required to consult each other at least once every school year about arrangements for admission, to consider whether they are satisfactory and before publishing arrangements for future admissions.

Where the LEA is responsible for admissions, it may set a higher figure for admissions than the standard number established under the 1988 Education Reform Act, provided that the governors have been consulted and the school has the physical capacity. However, the standard number may not be reduced without the consent of the Secretary of State following a Public Notice procedure. Governors may ask the LEA to increase the standard number for their school; if the LEA refuses and disagreement persists then the governors may refer the matter to the Secretary of State for resolution. Similar provisions apply where the governors are responsible for admissions in voluntary aided schools.

Appeals

The law gives parents the right to express preferences over admissions and obliges local authorities and governors to give effect to those preferences wherever possible. Local authorities and governors go to great lengths to accommodate parents' wishes in allocating school places and in subsequent mediation and discussions where problems over admission have arisen. There will still be cases, however, where parents have not obtained a place at their preferred school.

Under the 1980 Education Act, local education authorities, and governors of aided and special agreement schools, are required to establish appeal committees to which parents may turn if they are dissatisfied with an admissions decision. The decisions of appeal committees are binding on the LEA or governors who set them up, and also on the governors of any county or controlled school which an LEA appeal committee decides should admit a child. Governors sometimes feel that an authority may not be acting as they would wish over admissions, possibly allowing in too many pupils, or too few, or failing to keep a proper balance of numbers between all the schools in a concentrated urban area. The pattern of appeal committee decisions since the 1980 Act, and more particularly case law and Ombudsman reports on admission arrangements, make it clear that it is the responsibility of the LEA to 'prove its case' where there has been an appeal against a refusal to meet a parental preference. The LEA must first demonstrate that it has properly applied the standard number for admissions and then that it has fully considered the case of the individual child in the light of the published criteria for admissions.

If there are places available in the school in an appropriate age group, and if the child has the necessary ability when admission is determined by ability, an authority must admit the child if the parent so wishes or be extremely careful that any refusal to admit is on absolutely reasonable grounds. Where parents are dissatisfied with the decision of an appeal committee, they may take their case to the Secretary of State, to the Ombudsman or Council on Tribunals or to the civil law. The LEA, or the governors if they are responsible, should not normally offer admission to a child after an appeal has been denied unless there has been a material change in circumstances, for example vacancies arising at a school within its standard number because other children decide not to take up places offered to them.

Publication of information

Section 8 of the 1980 Act requires every local education authority annually to publish a prospectus for each school. In many authorities, the preparation of information about county schools is undertaken by the governors and head teachers on behalf of the authority. This information goes beyond the detail immediately relevant to admission such as the number of pupils to be admitted annually and admission criteria, and is intended to provide all parents with a comprehensive view of the school's objectives and policies. Amongst the information to be included is the following:

(a)   the curriculum for different age groups;
(b)   pastoral care and careers information;
(c)   policy regarding homework;
(d)   general arrangements for school discipline;
(e)   range of societies and activities;
(f)   dress and school uniform;
(g)   examination entry policies and results.

It is intended to add information on absence rates from September 1992.

This is an opportunity for schools to establish from the outset a dialogue with their parents. It is important that schools should do what they can to explain their aims and policies to parents and thus associate them with their work. Governors have a vital role to play in ensuring that there is effective communication between the school and its parents from this early stage and throughout a child's career.

Role of governors

Governors, then, should:

1. Ascertain and understand clearly the functions and duties which apply to them under the status of the school and the arrangements in their local education authority.
2. If they have responsibility for admissions, exercise those functions most scrupulously in exact conformity with the admissions procedures laid down.
3. If they do not have responsibility for admissions, avoid any exercise or implied exercise of powers vested solely in the LEA.

4. Be aware that decisions taken by the governors in relation to the admission of pupils to the school may be challenged by reference to an appeal committee set up under the 1980 Education Act whose decision is binding on the governors. If an appeal committee determines that a child be offered a place at the school, the governors must admit the child. Such decisions are similarly binding on the LEA.
5. Use every opportunity that can be found to establish and develop effective communication and relationship between the school and the parents of its pupils.

Governors will find that where they have responsibility for admissions, or are approached by parents about admissions, they can be faced with difficult decisions and consequent parental dissatisfaction. Often, the case of an individual family, pressing their claim for admission with great force or in distress, can seem very compelling, but many other families may also have strong claims but less well argued. Governors should be careful that they do not allow sympathy for one family, personal interests or friendships, to intrude upon a decision making process that must be administered objectively and fairly, and may well be open to public scrutiny.

6
Finance

The LEA has the duty to provide the whole of its area with an efficient system of education. It must also provide the money necessary for doing so. School governors have the duty of ensuring that within the school each child is offered the opportunities for education suitable to his or her age, ability, aptitude and any special needs and that resources are adequately deployed to achieve this.

In reality, prior to the 1988 Education Reform Act, and except for some provisions in the 1986 Education Act on governors' powers over revenue expenditure, governors had little significant direct control of, or responsibility for, finance within schools.

Local Management of Schools (LMS)

The provisions of the 1988 Education Reform Act dealing with school finance and staffing have brought about a fundamental change in the relationship between LEAs and schools. The requirement to introduce schemes for the Local Management of Schools brought major new powers and responsibilities for governors. This chapter is concerned with the provisions for finance and associated financial issues and procedures. However, so fundamental is the impact of LMS that its consequences and implications will be felt in other areas and there are important references in later chapters, particularly those on staffing, premises and special needs.

Indeed, it is important to place the financial provisions of LMS within the wider contents and intentions of the 1988 Act. Financial provision to primary and secondary schools is to depend largely on pupil numbers. Pupil numbers will be subject to 'more open enrolment' and greater achievement of parental choice in school admissions. In the introduction and implementation of the National Curriculum and associated assessment requirements, schools will be required to give critical consideration to financial and staffing priorities. Governors will have responsibility for the cost of staff but also powers of appointment and dismissal in the light of their priorities. Schools will be expected to demonstrate their effectiveness publicly through such means as the annual report to parents including the financial statement, publication of examination results and attendance rates, and, in effect, through success in recruiting pupils which will in turn lead to additional funding. It is therefore quite appropriate that the earlier use of the term 'Local Financial Management' has been replaced by the all embracing concept of Local Management of Schools.

It is important to stress some basic distinctions within the financial provisions of LMS. First, there are two financial elements: the delegation of funds to schools covered by the LMS scheme with associated devolved powers for governors, and the determination of the amount of those funds by means of formula funding with a public statement on how that formula works. Secondly, LMS does not of itself alter the total amount of money available within an LEA for the purposes of the school system, but it will have the inevitable effect of greater scrutiny and debate of that total finance and how it is used.

Further, the introduction of LMS has not changed the existing sources of LEA income which remain central government grant, the proceeds of the community charge and miscellaneous income including rents, fees, sales and gifts. The balance between central government grant and locally raised finance has shifted considerably in recent years and the mechanism for some local form of revenue raising remains the subject of unresolved controversy. LEA total finances are very much subject to the annual White Paper, *The Government's Expenditure Plans*, and macro-economic policies and controls. In addition, there has been an increasing tendency for funding to LEAs from central government to be channelled through specific schemes such as the Technical and Vocational Education Initiative and Grants for Education Support and Training for particular nominated projects. Thus, both the total amount of finance available to the individual LEA and specific areas within that total are constrained. It is against this background that the LEA must devolve funds to governing bodies and consider the use of funds still held centrally by the LEA for the education service.

All LEAs are obliged by the 1988 Education Reform Act to submit LMS schemes to the DES for the approval of the Secretary of State following consultation with governors and heads of schools covered by the scheme. Monitoring of schemes once they are in place and any significant changes will involve continuing consultation.

All secondary schools and primary schools are to be subject to LMS. Nursery schools are excluded but special schools are to be funded by formula from 1st April, 1994. There are stages in the required timetable for implementation, and for the phasing out of any agreed transitional provisions, but all primary and secondary schools must have received delegated budgets by 1st April, 1994.

As a result of the introduction of LMS, the role of the LEA in school finance has become more strategic and has moved away from detailed financial responsibility and control within individual schools. The LEA has the duty to determine the total resources available to the schools it maintains and the formula through which delegation of those funds is made. It is responsible for establishing financial regulations for the exercise of devolved powers by governors, monitoring the performance of schools and, potentially, for the operation of sanctions including the withdrawal of delegation. Until a school has delegated powers, the LEA will exercise appropriate financial management. Implicit in these duties are significant requirements to provide advice, support and training for governors and head teachers and to ensure that the Education Department is structured and staffed to provide that support and an effective and efficient service to schools operating under delegated powers. As experience of LMS develops, so key issues and difficulties may arise which will require a continuing framework to secure arrangements for consultation and any variation of the scheme.

The governing body will have the responsibility for the running of the school within the delegated budget, subject to the provisions of the authority's LMS scheme and national statutory requirements. The DES has emphasised these requirements and the extended powers of governors in a series of publications targeted directly to governors. Governors will need to consider carefully aims, objectives and priorities within the school and how available resources may best be deployed to meet these. Clearly, they will require extensive consultation with the head teacher so that they may take his or her advice and, in a large school, that of the senior management team. It will be important to develop a management plan which relates aims and objectives to the finance available so that the curricular needs of the school and its pupils are fully considered and plans established to achieve the best possible provision. Staffing and premises-related expenses are inevitably major items, and areas where governors' new powers and responsibilities are very apparent. Careful planning to meet both short and longer term targets will be essential, with prudent use of virement between budget headings and maintenance of reasonable contingencies to meet the unexpected.

The governing body may properly delegate some powers and decisions to the head teacher. They may also wish to appoint a sub-committee to deal with financial matters, subject to proper and clear arrangements for membership and decision taking. It is not possible to establish hard and fast guidelines for these kinds of financial delegation. Much will depend on the size of the school, local circumstances and the particular stage of development in the school, and governors will need to make arrangements appropriate to their circumstances. What is clear is the expectation that governors will be much more fully involved not just in financial details but in financial planning to fulfil all their responsibilities.

In any LEA, governors should familiarise themselves with the details of their local scheme of LMS, the dates for the implementation of various stages, the opportunities for in-service training and the mechanism for continuing consultation over the development of the scheme and its details. What follows is a general description of the statutory framework for LMS schemes and guidance on some issues which commonly give rise to concern.

For each financial year the LEA must determine the General Schools Budget. This comprises all the LEA's expenditure on schools within the LMS scheme including funds to be devolved, central costs in the Education Department and the costs of services provided for education by other local authority departments and any sums held for contingencies or inflation during the financial year.

The LEA is able to retain from the General Schools Budget finance for mandatory exceptions (that is areas of expenditure which the Secretary of State does not allow to be delegated) and discretionary exceptions (that is areas of expenditure where the Secretary of State permits either delegation or central management of funds).

Mandatory exceptions comprise capital expenditure, that is spending on new buildings and major areas of equipment, including repayments and interest on borrowing, and specific government grant schemes. Such schemes include Grants for Education Support and Training (GEST), Section 11 Grants, Travellers' Children Grants and the Technical and Vocational Education Initiative (TVEI). Usually, the LEA has to make a contribution from its own funds as a condition of receiving such grants.

Discretionary exceptions include such items as:

— central administrative costs in the LEA (as well as other local authority department charges for education services)
— home to school transport
— school meals service
— structural repairs and maintenance
— insurance for premises and equipment
— statemented pupils and special education support services
— educational psychologists
— education welfare officers
— pupil benefits, e.g. clothing or maintenance grants
— school crossing patrols
— schools' music service
— schools' library service
— LEA curriculum initiatives
— dismissal, redundancy and premature retirement payments which fall on the LEA
— special staff costs, e.g. safeguarding of allowances and elements of supply cover which arise in unusual circumstances
— contingencies to meet emergencies or unexpected and large increases in pupil numbers
— contracts which have already been let under competitive tendering legislation.

The sum which remains after the deduction from the General Schools Budget of capital expenditure, specific grants, home to school transport, school meals and transitional items is called the Potential Schools Budget. The balance of the General Schools Budget after removing all the exceptions is called the Aggregated Schools Budget and this must be devolved to individual schools according to the LMS formula in the authority.

The Secretary of State has indicated that from April 1993 he will require LEAs to delegate to schools at least 85% of the Potential Schools Budget. By the same date at least 80% of the Aggregated Schools Budget must be directly related to pupil numbers.

Governors will generally, therefore, find themselves responsible for all staff costs, day to day premises costs including non-structural repairs and maintenance, fuel and energy costs, all supplies and services used by the school including books, equipment, stationery, examination fees, telephones and postage and some elements of insurance. The precise areas of responsibility should be identified in the local LMS scheme.

Some LMS issues

It is in the area of discretionary exceptions that debate about the development of LMS continues to be very active. The question is whether certain services should necessarily be funded directly by the LEA in pursuit of its statutory duties and because they can be more efficiently and effectively organised as central services, or whether there is scope for further delegation to school level. For example, it may be argued that the scale and complexities of home to school travel, not least for pupils entitled to free travel, are such that it is better organised by the LEA. Functions such as personnel services and payment of salaries require levels of expertise and management systems which may be better provided on an authority wide basis. Pupils with statements of special educational needs have particular statutory rights involving detailed procedures and specialist staff, such as educational psychologists, which may best be provided for and protected as whole authority activities. On the other hand, there are arguments that schools with additional delegated funds could take responsibility for 'buying in' additional or specialist services and support.

The cost of central administration, including inspectors and advisers, has become a focus of particular attention, not least because of the redefinition of the LEA's role in strategic terms and the ability of schools to acquire grant maintained status. In that case, schools receive funding direct from the Department of Education and Science including a figure to compensate for the loss of LEA services.

The formula for the allocation of the Aggregated Schools Budget is clearly of considerable importance and interest to governors and they will need to be conversant with the formula applying in their authority. For primary and secondary schools, the Secretary of State has said that he expects the formula to be clear and explicit, predictable in the outcome of its application, based on objective needs rather than historical spending patterns and largely determined by pupil numbers. LEAs may introduce weighting for pupils of different ages, special consideration for small schools and provision for special educational needs. They may introduce other variables but not to such an extent that the formula becomes over complex or that the basic principle of overall equity is lost.

The formula should apply to both primary and secondary schools. (Guidance on extending LMS to special schools recognises the very different context of those schools and suggests a formula based more on types of pupil need rather than pupil numbers).

Some general concerns have commonly arisen about formulae and their operation. The formula is based on LEA average salary costs yet each school's average salaries will vary according to the experience of its staff; this may have a considerable financial impact where LEA and school averages are significantly different. Many schemes allow for a transitional period of adjustment in this major area of expenditure. School premises vary enormously in age, size, type of construction and condition; even height above sea level can be a significant factor. Some authorities have tried to introduce variable weightings for such factors but this can lead to great complications without resolving concerns between schools about equity of treatment. The protection of small schools, whatever definition of small is adopted, for curriculum purposes can be a controversial matter which skews the distribution of the Aggregated Schools Budget. More generally, the introduction of LMS has had a considerable impact on clerical and administrative support staff and functions in schools which requires both training and the introduction of appropriate information technology systems for school administration and finance. Finally, there is a heavy demand on LEA education departments to produce regular and reliable financial information and statements for schools in a form which they will find useful and workable.

LEAs will generally include in their LMS schemes impartial advice and guidelines. These are likely to include broad issues such as good personnel practice, regard for special educational needs and adherence to guidelines on value for money and health and safety. Specific financial conditions may apply to the keeping and audit of accounts, provision of information to the LEA, handling of deficits and surpluses between financial years, entering into long term financial commitments, capital and leasing activity, banking, (including new provisions on school cheque books), purchasing conditions, competitive tendering, disposal of equipment and related matters. The intention of the Secretary of State is that such conditions should strike a reasonable balance between the local freedom of governing bodies and the overall duties of the LEA with proper regard to probity and the proper use of public funds.

Monitoring the effectiveness of schools under LMS is an important consideration for LEAs and will increasingly become an aspect of inspection and review of schools as a whole, emphasising the connection between effective curriculum provision and the personnel and financial planning required to achieve the best possible outcomes. A framework for monitoring and evaluation of schools should be a feature of the LMS scheme.

Other financial issues

Governors should be clear about the arrangements for insurance within the local LMS scheme, including insurance for premises and equipment losses under various circumstances, legal liability towards staff, parents, pupils, visitors and helpers, cash and fidelity guarantees and pupil activities. In some cases, there may be a division of responsibility between governors and the local authority over the cost of premiums.

Under the 1988 Education Reform Act governors are not personally liable for the consequences of action taken 'in good faith'. Such a phrase can only be tested ultimately in the courts but where governors are unsure or anxious about their liability in a particular case they may wish to seek advice from the LEA.

Another potentially difficult area is that of gifts and private school funds. School funds and donations have increased markedly in size in recent years. They are legitimate and useful to schools but require particularly careful handling and accounting to avoid any misunderstanding with parents or the community. The deployment of such funds might well be the subject of discussion with parent groups. Gifts of equipment or even additional buildings and facilities also require careful and tactful consideration. For example, minibuses, major items of equipment and swimming pools may have significant on going revenue, maintenance and, ultimately, replacement costs. Equipment or buildings may have implications for LEA premises responsibilities which will need to be cleared in advance. Again, discussions between governors and parent groups may be helpful in avoiding misunderstanding or later difficulties.

Governors and LEAs will need to draw up policies in respect of charging pupils for any activities and the arrangements for remitting such charges. Such policies must be within the overall legal context for charging for school activities and distinguish between cases where the activity is paid for by the governors and the LEA.

Under the 1988 Local Government Act, LEA services in cleaning, grounds maintenance, school catering and repair and maintenance of vehicles became subject to competitive tendering. Competitive tendering for building maintenance under earlier legislation was also implemented. LEAs will often have made contract arrangements for these services before or during the implementation of LMS. The LMS scheme must make clear to governors the interaction of such arrangements with the assumption of delegated powers by governors under LMS and the options available at the end of these contracts.

In general, governors will be able to choose whether to join in contract arrangements made by the LEA or to make their own arrangements. If they choose to make their own arrangements they will need to understand and follow the procedures in the Local Government Act on competitive tendering. Where schools stay within an LEA arranged contract they will be able to choose the standard of service specification which they require.

Aided and special agreement schools

The provisions of LMS apply, generally, to governors of voluntary aided and special agreement schools as they do to governors of county and voluntary controlled schools. The major areas of difference are found in responsibilities for school premises and grounds and are dealt with in another chapter. It is not uncommon for voluntary schools to have access to foundation or charitable funds which may be subject to particular conditions. Otherwise, the advice on private funds and gifts in county schools might well apply. Voluntary schools may have a particular source of additional advice and guidance in the national bodies maintained by the Churches. The general rule should be that where a financial activity or additional provision may impact on the responsibilities of the LEA then there should be prior discussion.

Competitive tendering does not apply to voluntary aided school employees except where an element of the workforce is employed by the LEA. A common example would be the school meals staff and in such a case competitive tendering requirements do apply.

Audit Commission

The Audit Commission, though established by government, is an independent body which is required to ensure that authorities have made proper arrangements to secure economy, efficiency and effectiveness in the use of resources. In addition to local audit activity and management advice, the Commission has produced a number of significant national reports on ways of achieving better LEA management in education, including secondary education, the removal of surplus places and home to school transport. The Commission makes comments to central as well as local government and has, for example, drawn attention to difficulties in local authority management arising from central government policy and practice in capital expenditure, school reorganisation and teachers' pay and conditions. Although an advisory, not an executive body, the Audit Commission has become an important voice in the consideration of the management of education.

7
Conduct and curriculum of the school

The duty of governors to exercise a general oversight of the conduct and curriculum of the school is perhaps their most fundamental duty, outweighing even their responsibility for the management of the school's budget. At the same time, it is the one which is most difficult to understand. As the question of the curriculum is at the centre of a vigorous national debate which touches upon many sensitive areas, it is important for governors to be clear as to their own role and as to the role and responsibilities of others. This chapter is, therefore, designed to clarify the governors' duties, particularly in the light of the 1986 and 1988 Education Acts, and to give guidance concerning the exercise of those duties.

Conduct of the school

Section 16 of the 1986 Education Act established the general principle that for all schools the conduct of the school should be under the direction of the governing body, subject to the statutory responsibilities of others. That duty lies at the heart of the work of the governing body as the guarantor of the school's identity. It enables the governors to exercise an important influence over the ethos of the school, and on many other matters which affect the school's success. It enables them to concern themselves with the school's contribution to the life of the local community. It also enables the governing body to have a voice in many important matters where responsibility rests mainly or partly with the LEA or the head teacher.

School curriculum
Background to current curriculum debate

For many years after the 1944 Act, the curriculum of schools was defined in the broadest terms. The curriculum had to be such as to provide efficient education for the individual child within the context of the community. Beyond a general requirement that education should be suited to the needs of the child, secular education was not defined either with the clarity with which the requirements for religious education are laid down, nor with the material conditions relating to physical education. It was, therefore, open to the local authorities to interpret secular education as widely or as narrowly as they pleased. In practice, the expectation has been that the schools would deal with and provide an ever broadening spectrum of education. That education, whatever its precise nature, has to be given at least in part by instruction and training, and has to include provision for practical instruction.

The practical interpretation of these broad requirements, especially in view of new situations created, for example, by the raising of the school leaving age, was extremely difficult, and highlighted the extent to which control of the curriculum continued effectively to be the province of the teachers and, in particular, of the head teacher.

This situation was reinforced, perhaps inadvertently, by the setting up in 1964 of the Schools Council to promote and encourage curriculum study and development. The majority of the members of the Schools Council were teachers. Subsequently the Schools Council was disbanded and replaced in part by the Schools Curriculum Development Committee whose constitution was based on a much broader representation. Most recently, of course, the government has established a National Curriculum Council with representatives from Higher Education, Business or Industry and with only a minority who are serving teachers.

A further optional element of the secondary school curriculum was added by the Education (Work Experience) Act 1973 which enabled 'local education authorities to arrange for children to have work experience as part of their education in the last year of compulsory schooling'.

The changing circumstances of our society in the 1970s were reflected in increased attention being focused on the schools, their management, and the social relevance of the content of education. The Taylor Committee, set up in 1975 to review the arrangements for the management and government of primary and secondary schools in England and Wales, summarised much of the debate in this sensitive area in the report *A New Partnership for our Schools*. They found that different people meant different things by the 'curriculum', but made two significant statements. First, recognising the need to define the aims of schools, they quoted the following statement of aims from a paper prepared by the DES in 1976:

1. To enable children to acquire the basic skills of literacy, oracy and numeracy, and to stimulate their curiosity and imagination.
2. To enable them to acquire the basic knowledge, practice in skills and in reasoning to equip them to enter a world of work which is becoming increasingly sophisticated in its processes and techniques, which is competitive and which is likely to demand the ability to adapt oneself to learn new processes from time to time.
3. To leave the children at the end of their period of compulsory schooling with an appetite for acquiring further knowledge, experience and skills at different periods in later life; and able to benefit from additional education to a variety of levels.
4. To prepare them to live and work with others in adult life; and to develop attitudes enabling them to be responsible members of the community.
5. To help them develop aesthetic responsibility and appreciation, and skills and interests for leisure time.
6. To mitigate the educational disadvantages that many children suffer through poor home conditions, limited ability or serious physical or mental handicap.

Secondly, they stated:

> Our preferred concept of the school curriculum effectively comprehends the sum of experiences to which a child is exposed at school.

The curriculum issue was put into even sharper focus by the speech of the then Prime Minister, Mr James Callaghan, at Ruskin College in 1976 and by the 'Great Debate' which followed. That discussion has continued, involving not only the DES, local education authorities, parents and educational bodies, but also, and increasingly, industry and training organisations.

Concern for the effective application of curricular policies prompted the government in 1981, following the publication of *The School Curriculum* to encourage, through the issue of DES Circular 6/81, the further development of expressly formulated curricular policies at the local level. DES Circular 8/83 followed up this initiative by asking each LEA to provide a report on the progress made in drawing up a policy for the curriculum in its primary and secondary schools including a description of the roles played in this process by those within and beyond the Education Service, and a statement of the ways in which the policy was to be given practical effect.

Addressing the North of England Conference in Sheffield in January 1984, Sir Keith Joseph, the then Secretary of State for Education and Science, proposed a programme of measures which was related to the school curriculum in the interest of raising standards. He took the view that there was widespread agreement as to the need to improve the standards achieved by pupils and that broad national agreement about the objectives and content of the school curriculum was a necessary step towards the improvement.

Better Schools (1985) summarised the allocation of functions for the secular curriculum, subsequently formalised in the 1986 Education Act, in the following terms:

(i)   the LEA will be responsible for formulating and implementing the curricular policy for its area;

(ii)   the governing body will have a duty to determine a statement of the school's curricular aims and objectives, and to review it from time to time. In doing so, it will be required to seek the advice of the head teacher and to consult the LEA;

(iii)   the head teacher will be responsible for the organisation and delivery of the curriculum, including detailed syllabuses and the teaching approaches and materials employed within the available resources and having regard to the statement of aims and objectives determined by the governing body;

(iv)   the curricular arrangements for pupils who are the subject of statements under the 1981 Education Act will be determined by the terms of the statement.

The objective within the relevant sections of the Act was to define the various responsibilities so that each party was clear about the role it had to play but, at the same time, to distribute the functions in such a way that the views of all concerned could find expression, and that there would be no imposition of the views of any one party. Ideally, this corporate approach would lead to a curriculum, which had the necessary breadth, balance and relevance to meet the needs of pupils in a particular school.

The National Curriculum

The 1988 Education Reform Act moved the curriculum debate a major step forward. The Act begins by maintaining the general approach in that it requires all maintained schools for pupils aged 5–16 to provide

a balanced and broadly based curriculum which:
(a) promotes the spiritual, moral, cultural, mental and physical development of pupils at the school and of society; and
(b) prepares such pupils for the opportunities, responsibilities and experiences of adult life.

It is now for the governing body to determine the curriculum for the school in the light of the LEA's published policy on the type of curriculum to be provided in maintained schools in its area. However, the school's curriculum must include provision for religious education and collective worship, along with the National Curriculum for every registered pupil of compulsory school age.

In the 1988 Education Reform Act, for the first time the nature and content of a National Curriculum is specified. It comprises three core subjects, English, Mathematics and Science, and seven other foundation subjects, History, Geography, Technology (including Design), a modern foreign language at secondary level, Art, Music and Physical Education. Although the manner in which the curriculum will be taught is a matter for individual schools, the content is determined by the Secretary of State through his approval for each subject area of the attainment targets setting out what children should be expected to know and be able to do in up to ten levels of increasing difficulty, and the programmes of study for what they must be taught in order to reach these targets. He will also determine the assessment arrangements which will demonstrate pupils' progress against the attainment targets at the end of the four Key Stages, corresponding to ages 7, 11, 14 and 16. Records will be kept showing each pupil's progress and attainment in terms of the ten levels.

The process of implementing the National Curriculum in full is a lengthy one as can be seen from the table below:

			KS1	KS2	KS3	KS4
Mathematics	Introduced	Autumn	1989	1990	1989	1992
and Science	First assessed	Summer	1991	1994	1992	1994
English	Introduced	Autumn	1989	1990	1990	1992
	First assessed	Summer	1991	1994	1993	1994

| Technology | Introduced | Autumn | 1990 | 1990 | 1990 | 1993 |
	First assessed	Summer	1992	1994	1993	1995
History and	Introduced	Autumn	1991	1991	1991	1994
Geography	First assessed	Summer	1993	1995	1994	1996
Modern	Introduced	Autumn			1992	1995
Foreign	First assessed	Summer			1995	1997
Language						
Art, Music	Introduced	Autumn	1992	1992	1992	1995
and Physical	First assessed	Summer	1994	1996	1995	1997
Education						

Some changes have already been made to the original plan, for example, in that History and Geography should be alternatives after age 14, unless short courses are taken, in which case both subjects would be studied; and that Art and Music should be optional after age 14. Until the detailed requirements have been introduced for all subjects, pupils aged 5–14 have to study all the foundation subjects 'for a reasonable time' during each Key Stage.

The governing body shares responsibility with the LEA and the head for ensuring that the National Curriculum is followed. This includes making sure that enough lesson time is provided for pupils to cover the curriculum, and that only approved external qualifications and syllabuses are offered to pupils.

Other curriculum considerations

A school's curriculum does not, however, have to be confined to the basic curriculum so far described. Depending on the abilities and aptitudes of their pupils, most secondary schools will seek to include a number of other subject areas, normally for examination at 16. Recent national and local initiatives in the field of vocational education and training, centring particularly on the 14–18 age range, and embracing the work of schools and colleges of further education and the needs of industry and commerce, have brought an important enrichment of curriculum opportunity and delivery for many pupils. The course content and teaching methods promoted within the Technical and Vocational Education Initiative have developed personal qualities and positive attitudes towards work as well as a wide range of competence and, generally, a more practical approach throughout the curriculum. Many secondary and primary schools will also be looking to introduce opportunities for promoting cross curricular themes such as environmental education, personal and social education, and economic and business awareness.

How can governors exercise their responsibilities for the curriculum?

To reconcile the requirement to provide each individual child with an education suitable to his particular needs, while at the same time meeting the diverse and changing needs of the community, is a formidable task. If, indeed, the curriculum is the whole educational policy of the school, then most issues affecting the conduct of the school arise from the curriculum itself. Without an understanding of the educational policy of the school, the governors cannot fulfil their functions. Such understanding is fundamental. Practical implementation of the policy is so complex that only those charged with the constant day to day task of carrying it out can effectively undertake the necessary detailed work. What children are finally asked to learn in the classroom, how the processes of learning are conducted, and how resources are used to teach, are matters which are almost exclusively within the competence of the head and staff of the school.

All this must, however, be within the broad limits of what is socially and morally acceptable. Transgression of such limits is held to reflect adversely on the governors whose oversight of the curriculum is consequently deemed to have been inadequately exercised. Consultation with the head and full information from the head are the essential ingredients of good oversight of the curriculum by the governors. Governors can never hope to know the needs of individual children, but their experience can be invaluable in a partnership which keeps under review the aims and policy at the school to ensure their relevance to the complex of needs which the school must satisfy.

This is all the more so when the curriculum is seen to include what is commonly referred to as 'the hidden curriculum' — all those elements which constitute the ethos of the school — through which the school makes its contribution to the development of the community. As these elements cannot be prescribed or taught in programme detail, an awareness of their reality cannot be transmitted to governors by reports; only by experience and direct contact with the school can such awareness be achieved. To this end, governors should take full advantage of their responsibilities on more formal occasions such as, for example, the appointment of staff, to deepen their knowledge of the school. They will have the opportunity of participating in the more ceremonial occasions in the school calendar, but schools also welcome visits from governors during working sessions. Indeed, many schools will create situations by which governors become involved in the life of the school, not merely as fund-raisers. The deeper the understanding of the school shown by governors, the greater will be their capacity to support the school, and the greater will be the school's appreciation of the governing body.

Perhaps there is no task more difficult than that of recognising and giving to young people the highest standards of living by which the community regulates or should regulate its civilised activity. Governors have a vital contribution to make in what is a serious and exacting role. A deep, informed and sensitive understanding between governors and head in this area is likely to contribute tremendously to the growth of a good school. As HM Inspectors say:

> definitions cannot improve standards or guarantee quality; but greater clarity and agreement about aims and objectives can provide a better base for evaluation and hence for more effective action.

Responsibility for the conduct and curriculum of the school, in consultation with the head, requires governors to be well-informed and constantly caring and vigilant about standards. The articles of government provide for the governing body to have power to review their conclusions about curriculum matters whenever they think fit, but it is their duty to do so immediately following any major reorganisation of the school, such as a transfer of the school to a new site, a reorganisation which involves the establishment, or an alteration or discontinuance of schools in accordance with Sections 12 or 13 of the 1980 Act. The curriculum should be a living element within the school, and it is the task of the governors to ensure that it is constantly under review and changing to meet new demands.

Religious Education and collective worship

All county and controlled schools must provide religious education for all pupils (apart from those withdrawn by their parents) as part of the basic curriculum. In county schools, this will be in accordance with the Agreed Syllabus for the area which is monitored by a Standing Advisory Council on Religious Education (SACRE) involving representatives of the Church of England, other religious groups, teachers and the LEA. The SACRE can require the LEA to set up a Statutory Conference to review the Agreed Syllabus. As a rule, controlled schools also follow the Agreed Syllabus although the law allows for religious education according to any provisions in the school's trust deed should parents request it. All county and controlled schools must also provide daily collective worship for all pupils apart from those withdrawn by their parents. Following the 1988 Education Reform Act the collective worship required in a county school must be 'wholly or mainly of a broadly Christian character', although there are provisions for this to be disapplied for schools where the religious affiliation of the pupils makes it inappropriate. The governing body shares responsibility with the head and the LEA for ensuring that these requirements are met.

This is a delicate area in which governors have to exercise their functions, not least because of the personal beliefs and views of teachers who may require to have some involvement in this area of the curriculum. There may well be governors who hold equally strong opinions. The first point to be made is that a governor's personal view must not obscure his duty to see, by exercising his responsibilities for the curriculum, that the law requiring religious instruction is carried out. The second duty of governors is to satisfy themselves that the requirement to give religious education is fulfilled with the maximum efficiency of which the school is capable.

Sex education

In the course of public debate during the passage of the 1986 Education Act, particular attention was given to sex education in schools. The outcome was that the governing body, when considering the LEA's statement of its curriculum policy, must determine whether sex education should form part of the curriculum of the school. It will have a duty to ensure that where it is, it is given in such a manner 'as to encourage the pupils to have due regard to moral considerations, and the value of family life'. The governors must keep a written statement of their policy on this, which must, at the same time, be subject to any requirements of the National Curriculum.

Political education

It is a fundamental principle that teachers should avoid bias and personal prejudice in their teaching, endeavouring to present issues in a balanced context. This is particularly important in the field of politics and clauses were included in the 1986 Education Act to ensure this. It is the responsibility of the LEA and the governing body and head teacher of any county, voluntary or special school to forbid the pursuit of partisan political activities by any of the pupils who are junior pupils and the promotion of partisan political views in the teaching of any subject in the school. There is a similar responsibility in respect of all schools to take such steps as are reasonably practicable to ensure that where political issues are raised the pupils are offered a balanced presentation of opposing views.

Complaints about the curriculum

Parents do not have the right to withdraw their children from any aspect of the secular curriculum. The governing body has the discretion to allow parents to withdraw their children from any sex education provided which goes beyond the National Curriculum requirements, but it is not obliged to do so. The governing body has no discretion to allow parents to withdraw children from National Curriculum requirements other than in those circumstances described elsewhere in the book where parts of the curriculum may be modified or disapplied because of a pupil's special educational needs.

Parents are entitled, however, to have access to a formal appeal or complaints procedure where they feel the head, governors, or LEA, are acting unreasonably in respect of aspects of the National Curriculum. The LEA is responsible for devising an approved complaints procedure. The first formal stage of this will require the governing body to consider complaints, with the complainants having the right of appeal to the LEA if they are still dissatisfied after this. The appeal may relate to the refusal of a head to modify or disapply the National Curriculum for a particular pupil, and the complaints might relate to failure to provide the National Curriculum in the school or for a child, to follow the law on charging for curricular activities, to offer any approved qualifications or syllabuses, or to provide religious education and daily collective worship.

While the availability of such procedures is important in principle, governors will, by their regular review of the curricular provision within the school, help to avoid the necessity for any complaints and, where they do arise, seek to resolve them informally without recourse to formal procedures.

8
Examinations, assessment and accountability

Concern about the effectiveness of the Education Service following James Callaghan's intervention focused attention on the performance of individual schools. That focus was reinforced in the White Paper *Better Schools* published in March 1985. How to evaluate that performance has been the subject of prolonged, and sometimes bitter, debate and argument. In seeking to exercise their general responsibility for the conduct of the school, governors will need to know how to assess, monitor and influence the quality of what is provided. This chapter looks at several aspects of these functions.

Examinations

External examinations taken at school have long been a major factor influencing a pupil's successful transition into employment or further and higher education. Reforms of the examination system, particularly at 16+ and in respect of vocational qualifications, together with the development of a system of pupil profiling, have led to examination results being seen as only a part of a comprehensive pupil record of achievement, attitudes and potential. Governors need to have a clear view of the methods of examination and assessment currently in use, and of the extent to which raw data from examination results can be interpreted and used, either to assess the performance of a pupil or of the school. Examinations properly designed within a syllabus can act as a stimulus to a pupil's performance in his studies, and governors should ensure that the examination policies within a school stimulate and increase opportunities rather than constrain them.

In *Better Schools*, the specific objectives of examinations were defined as follows:

(i)   to raise standards across the whole ability range;

(ii)   to support improvements in the curriculum and in the way in which it is taught;

(iii)   to provide clear aims for teachers and pupils to the benefit of both and of higher education and employers;

(iv)   to record proven achievement;

(v)   to promote the measurement of achievement based on what candidates know, understand, and can do;

(vi)   to broaden the studies of pupils in the fourth and fifth secondary years, and of sixth form students.

The following sections describe the main forms of external examination likely to come to the attention of school governors:

GCE 'A' (Advanced) level

'A' level is designed as a preparation for higher education and an entry qualification for professional training. It is intended for the most able secondary school pupils who will sit up to three, or occasionally four, subjects, usually at 18 years of age. Sixth form students studying 'A' levels have, traditionally, followed an intensive course over a narrow curriculum field.

From time to time there is national debate about whether it is possible to give greater breadth to a student's sixth form programme without prejudicing the depth or intensity of individual 'A' level studies. The debate remains to be resolved.

AS (Advanced Supplementary) level

In an endeavour to broaden the curriculum diet and retain the principles of breadth and balance in sixth form studies, the government introduced AS levels in 1987. These subjects, normally taken alongside 'A' level courses, involve about half the amount of teaching time of an 'A' level course spread over two years. These additional subjects are intended to contrast with, or complement, the main 'A' level studies, and retain a similar academic content and depth. The educational objectives of this new course were welcomed but many schools particularly those with small sixth forms find increasing difficulty in providing for their students a wide enough range of subjects and subject combinations from the growing number of post-16 options now becoming available.

International Baccalaureate

The International Baccalaureate is an examination course accepted as fulfilling university entrance requirements in most countries of the world. Students study six subjects including their own language, a modern foreign language, mathematics, science, art and music, and one from a group of subjects which includes history and geography. All students follow a further course which examines the relationship between knowledge and beliefs.

The course is demanding for students and costly to mount. Nonetheless it is an alternative approach to advanced sixth form studies which is attracting growing numbers of supporters.

GCSE (General Certificate of Secondary Education)

In 1988 after many years of debate and discussion, a new single examination at 16+ replaced 'O' levels and CSE. This major reform of the examining system came about because of widespread dissatisfaction with the previous arrangements, involving more than 20 separate examination boards, each awarding its own certificates, with many hundreds of subject titles and nearly 19,000 syllabuses causing confusion for pupils, parents and employers. 'O' level and CSE grades overlapped in a way that was not fully understood. Children either had to be divided into 'O' or CSE teaching groups at age 14, on criteria that were frequently difficult to identify, or had to be prepared within the same teaching group for what could be two very dissimilar examinations.

GCSE is administered by five regional examining groups. National criteria, with which all GCSE syllabuses and examinations must comply, are developed by the examining groups, and approved by the Secretaries of State on the advice of the School Examinations and Assessment Council (SEAC). These criteria ensure that syllabuses in given subjects have sufficient content in common, that the assessment is conducted according to common principles, and that pupils, parents and other users of examinations are better informed and have a clearer understanding of what a GCSE certificate attests. The national criteria place a new emphasis on oral and practical skills, on coursework, on reasoning, and on the application as well as the acquisition of knowledge and understanding.

There are differentiated questions and papers which relate to the differing abilities of pupils, giving all pupils an opportunity to show positive achievement within the examination. The seven grades awarded (A-G) thus reflect achievement rather than the simple concepts of pass or fail. The new examining groups, which are regionally based, and are constituted largely of local education authority, teacher, employer, and higher education representatives, co-operate within the forum of a Joint Council for GCSE.

Vocational courses

Examinations set by the City and Guilds of London Institute (CGLI), the Royal Society of Arts (RSA) and the Business and Technician Education Council (BTEC) are designed mainly for use in further education, but some courses are offered in schools. In particular these are:

— The Certificate in Pre-Vocational Education. This has been updated and enhanced and is now offered by CGLI. It provides a curriculum based around the acquisition of core skills and vocational elements in a variety of areas. There is a strong element of general education, an emphasis on transferable skills and a progressively sharpening vocational focus.

— RSA courses are offered in a wide variety of practical skills areas such as typing, word processing and IT, in languages and a variety of business-related subjects.

— BTEC National Diplomas are offered in a variety of vocational areas. They are equivalent in standard to 'A' levels (at National Vocational Qualification level III). BTEC First Diplomas have been available for schools to use from September 1991. They are offered in most of the same vocational areas and offer progression opportunities to BTEC Nationals. Both First and National courses are usually offered jointly with local colleges.

The government has recently proposed the introduction of an Ordinary and Advanced Diploma in schools. One aim of this is to promote equal status between academic and vocational qualifications. It is proposed that broadly the Ordinary Diploma would be awarded for students who have achieved 4+ GCSEs at Grades A-C or equivalent vocational qualifications which are to be developed. The Advanced Diploma would be awarded for the achievement of 2 'A' levels at Grades A-E, a BTEC National Diploma or other courses at NVQ level 3 or a combination of these.

Vocational qualifications are currently being written for the National Council for Vocational Qualifications (NCVQ) using competence-based criteria at four levels. All vocational courses will ultimately have to be approved by NCVQ; existing validating and examining bodies will continue to offer the courses.

Assessment

The notion of regular monitoring and assessment of pupil performance is not new. Indeed, it lies at the heart of effective teaching where assessment outcomes point to pupil strengths and weaknesses, and help inform the next stage of the pupil's learning programme. The value of such assessment is readily recognised by all teachers. Less enthusiasm has been shown for other uses to which assessment outcomes have sometimes been put, partly because results have been used to draw spurious comparisons between schools and partly because without moderation between teachers and schools, such comparative data has little statistical validity.

These issues were addressed within the 1988 Education Reform Act. Accompanying the National Curriculum was the requirement for pupils to be assessed at or near the end of each Key Stage — i.e. at ages 7, 11, 14 and 16 — for the purpose of ascertaining what they have achieved in relation to the attainment targets for that stage. The assessment arrangements differ according to the area of the curriculum and the Key Stage, but they are based principally on a process of teacher assessment across the Key Stage, with a review of each child's performance made and recorded towards the end of that period, and a series of standard assessment tasks (SATs) nationally compiled, and assessed or marked by the teachers against carefully determined national criteria. The assessments indicate the level at which each child is working in each subject on a 10 level scale which covers a normal progression from ages 5 to 16.

The programme for the full implementation of the National Curriculum and its associated assessment is an extended one, and it is likely to be near the end of the 1990s before the whole programme is in place. Extensive trialing of materials, either to support teacher assessment or for the SATs themselves, precedes the introduction of the formal assessment process for each subject at each Key Stage. It has become apparent that for the assessment process to be manageable for teachers, and for it not unreasonably to interrupt pupils' learning programmes, the whole exercise must be significantly slimmed down from the original concept.

The pattern that has been determined by the Secretary of State for assessment at age 7 is for teacher assessment in all subjects across all attainment targets, i.e. indicating the knowledge, skills and understanding which pupils of different abilities and maturities are expected to have by the end of the Key Stage, supported by formal assessment through SATs in English,

Mathematics, Science and, in due course, Technology. By a process of aggregation of scores, 'results' will be obtained which will then be reported to each pupil's parents. The arrangements for assessment at Key Stages 2 and 3 are still far from clear, but the Secretary of State has made it known that he expects the emphasis in the assessment tasks to lean as far as possible towards written tests rather than lengthy practical activities. At Key Stage 4, a relationship has been devised between the 10 level National Curriculum scale and the seven grades for GCSE.

Governors will be advised by the head from time to time about progress in the implementation of the National Curriculum and its assessment, but they will have a particular interest in the outcome of the assessments at Key Stages 2, 3 and 4, where there is a requirement that in addition to each pupil's results being passed to his parents, the aggregated results for the school must be published more widely in a determined form. The extent to which those results can or should be used for judgements on the performance or worth of a school is likely to be the subject of heated debate in coming years. At the very least, however, governors are entitled to expect the head to place the school's results in context for them, and to indicate the extent to which they might provide evidence of a school's performance and progress.

Inspection/Monitoring or evaluation

Following the 1986 Education Act, articles of government have required governors of every county, controlled and maintained special school to consider and produce regular statements on the aims of the secular curriculum for the school while the governors of every aided and special agreement school actually control the secular curriculum. The 1988 Education Reform Act extends that responsibility to ensuring the implementation of the National Curriculum and provision for religious education. In fulfilling these duties, governors will rely in great part on heads' reports; they will visit the schools themselves; they will increasingly receive the outcomes of the National Curriculum assessment, and in a secondary school, they will consider external examination results; and they will have the views of the local community. But from time to time, in the words of the Plowden Report (1967), 'Schools need inspection as well as advice'.

Inspection is not a function of a governing body — but to consider, debate and act on reports following inspection most certainly is. And their discussions on an inspection report will be the better if the governors know their school well. Their questioning of the reporting officer and of the head will then be more to the point and recommendations which they might wish to make as a consequence of the report are likely to be better informed.

Inspection may be:

1. By Her Majesty's Inspectors (HMI). These are appointed by the Queen in Counsel and have their headquarters in the Department of Education and Science, but they report as independent advisers to the Secretary of State. HMI now carry out inspections in a variety of forms. The most public is a general inspection of the whole school which is followed by a formal report presented to the governors and the authority, and subsequently published. Increasingly, inspections now take place across a number of schools covering some aspect of school life or curriculum. Reports may or may not be published, and schools will not always be individually named. Occasionally, HMI have undertaken an inspection of a local education authority through a sample survey of establishments and areas of the curriculum and service.

2. By local authority inspectors/advisers, either as routine or for a special purpose, for example to gather information on multi-racial education, on language teaching, or pastoral organisation.

3. Inspection of the work of a teacher by HMI or the advisers/inspectors of the local education authority.

HMI have complete discretion as to which school to inspect, although, in exceptional circumstances, they may be able to accede to an authority's request to inspect an institution where there is a particular problem. More usually, the response to a request of this nature is likely to be in the form of a pastoral visit.

The governors may ask the Chief Education Officer for an inspection, and, indeed, it is their right course of action if either they feel disquiet which no other discussion or investigation has allayed, or they wish to be better informed on some aspect of the school's life. The response to such a request may depend, to a large extent, on the availability of inspectorial/advisory resources, but authorities will usually endeavour to respond constructively to the concerns which have been articulated.

It cannot be too strongly stated, however, that if an inspection reveals or confirms a misgiving about an individual, and disciplinary action or even dismissal is contemplated, the requirements of the legislation and of the authority's approved procedures should be strictly followed. The governors have a responsibility to maintain the efficiency of the school; an individual has the right to safeguards laid down by law and good practice.

Most local education authorities will have set up programmes of monitoring and evaluation which are part of a continuous process which includes external assessment through school inspection, and self-evaluation through internal review. The development of a wide range of performance indicators for the school, to include, for example, examination results, pupil staying on rates post-16, absenteeism, staff turnover, will lead to a profile of school performance and effectiveness, and also identify targets which can support progress and development. Whatever system is used, it is vitally important that governors have at the front of their awareness a real concern for quality and improvement within the school for the sake of their own accountability to parents, and for the school's responsibility to the pupils.

There is currently much uncertainty about the form school inspection might take in the future in the light of recent government proposals. A review of HMI could well lead to that body having a greater responsibility for the quality of regular inspection of all educational establishments across the country. A proposal to remove from LEAs the obligation of inspecting schools and instead require governing bodies to contract with accredited inspection agencies to undertake formal inspections could place in jeopardy the very real improvement in the quality of establishments which is beginning to come about in large measure because of the way in which the inspection process is being used as a way of moving forward rather than simply reporting on what exists.

Accountability

The powers and duties conferred on governors by the articles of government have a single purpose, to enable the school to provide good, efficient and appropriate education for all the pupils registered at the school. Governors do not act in isolation or in total independence. They are part of the formal structures of society and are accountable for their actions in many ways.

Directly, governors are accountable to the community and to parents. By issuing information about the school and by presenting the governors' report to all parents annually the governors publicly offer an account of their operation for scrutiny and discussion. Governors are also responsible for the maintenance and transfer of pupils' educational records to which there are legal rights of access. The availability of minutes for inspection by parents and others similarly exposes the activities of the governing body to examination. To a lesser degree, consultation with their electing or appointment bodies fulfils a similar purpose. Subtly, discussion and public criticism could bring about modification of governing bodies' attitudes or actions, but the much more immediate sanction which the community, and parents in particular, can and do exercise is to express approval or disapproval of the governors' effectiveness by seeking admission for their children to the school or by sending them elsewhere.

The articles of government for every school must provide for the governing body to furnish to the local education authority such reports in connection with the discharge of their functions as the authority may require. The minutes must be open to inspection by the local education authority. Some duties may be carried out only after consultation with the local education authority, e.g. the making of a written statement as to the aims of the secular curriculum of the school. In financial matters, despite their increased discretion, the governors are accountable to the authority which would have the power to enforce corrective action if governors misused their powers, e.g. by overspending or by spending for inappropriate purposes.

Finally, governors are required to make reports and returns and give such information to the Secretary of State as he may require for the purpose of the exercise of his functions in relation to education.

9
Teaching and support staff

Nothing is more critical to the quality of a school than its staff and governors carry no more important responsibility than the selection and management of that precious resource. The increased professional demands and the developing staff shortages (especially in particular subject areas) have only intensified the need for governors to approach these responsibilities with the very greatest care, as errors have never been so expensive financially and educationally. It is an area where specialist personnel advice from within and outside the school can be of particular assistance to governors. Most education authorities will have recommended procedures for all the major staffing functions likely to be exercised by governors. The maintenance of effective staffing arrangements is a responsibility in which governor and local education authority co-operation is essential.

Recent years, particularly since the 1988 Education Reform Act, have seen a considerable shift in responsibility from the local education authority to the governors who now take all effective decisions relating to the appointment, remuneration and retention of staff. At the same time the duties required of heads and all teachers have been clarified and codified in a legal document *The Teachers' Pay and Conditions Document*, details of which are given in Appendix A.

Teaching staff

In a county, voluntary controlled or special agreement school teachers are the employees of the local education authority. In a voluntary aided school, they are the employees of the governors. However, in all schools it is for the governors to determine how many teachers shall be employed within the resources available. Clearly, governors' curriculum and staffing responsibilities dovetail. Governors should satisfy themselves that the distribution of posts within the school is appropriate for achieving the National Curriculum and other curricular aims which have been set.

Qualifications for appointment

It is the Secretary of State who is responsible for determining the entry requirements for teaching. Qualified teacher status can be achieved in a number of ways: by a four year course at an institution of Higher Education leading to a BEd. Degree; by a degree and a Post-Graduate Certificate in Education; by a degree and satisfaction of the requirements of the Articled Teachers' Scheme; by satisfying the requirements to become a Licensed teacher. EEC nationals who are recognised as qualified teachers in their own countries are granted qualified teacher status automatically on application to the Secretary of State. Other teachers trained overseas can be authorised by the DES provided that they meet the minimum requirements set out in DES Circular 13/91.

The Articled and Licensed Teachers' Schemes are relatively new. In brief, the Articled Scheme is a two year professional induction in which a graduate divides his or her time between the training institution and the school. The Licensed Scheme is open to those aged at least 24 and with at least two years' successful experience of higher education. Achievement of the Licence — and thus qualified teacher status — is normally after two years of satisfactory performance, during which the employer is expected to provide appropriate on-the-job training.

It is permitted to employ unqualified teachers should it prove impossible to appoint a qualified teacher to a post. Salary scales for unqualified staff are lower and before any such appointment is contemplated it must be clearly shown that there is no suitable qualified teacher available.

The Department of Education and Science maintains, and provides to each local education authority, List 99 — that is, the names of teachers not permitted to teach in maintained schools because of misconduct or criminal conviction. In addition, local education authorities are able to check police records in the case of any staff who will have access to children.

A teacher must satisfy a medical examination before being initially accepted for service and the local education authority will further require a satisfactory medical report on a teacher new to its service. All appointments are, therefore, made subject to a satisfactory medical report. The Secretary of State may after consultation with the local education authority or voluntary aided governors require the suspension or the termination of a teacher's employment on medical or educational grounds.

Some conditions will disqualify a teacher from employment, either for a limited period or permanently. Governors should check carefully that candidates are suitably qualified and eligible for appointment. Failure to do so can cause embarrassment on all sides and could leave the school understaffed in an important area.

Governors should make it clear that offers of appointment are, in the case of county and voluntary controlled schools, subject to confirmation by the local education authority. In the case of aided schools, the LEA is empowered to prohibit the appointment of a teacher who does not meet the contractual requirements.

Throughout the appointment procedure — shortlisting, interview and selection — governors should keep in mind the basic qualifications for a teaching post. It would not be proper to question a candidate for appointment in a county or voluntary controlled school about his or her religion. On the other hand, such questions would be admissible if candidates were seeking a post in a voluntary aided school or a post as reserved teacher in a voluntary controlled or special agreement school. Questions about the politics or union affiliation of candidates would be improper.

Traditionally in our education system, teachers have contributed to the whole development of children, both inside and outside the classroom, and not simply through the transmission of information and skills. It is, therefore, permissible to ask candidates about the contribution they would make to the wider life of the school, provided that governors have regard to the provisions of the Pay and Conditions Document.

Race Relations and Equal Opportunities Acts make it illegal for appointment bodies to consider the racial origin or, in the vast majority of cases, sex of applicants in determining their suitability for appointment. Governors should be very careful to ensure that candidates are considered solely on their individual suitability for the post in question.

Procedures for appointments

The process of appointment is now prescribed by the 1988

Education Reform Act. This gives the legal responsibility for all teacher appointments to the governors, with the LEA's role being to advise the governors and to confirm the appointment provided that it does not breach any relevant professional qualifications. It is a sign of a strong governing body that it is prepared to seek specialist advice over appointments and weigh that advice very carefully when reaching a decision.

Appointment of head teachers and deputy head teachers to county, controlled and special schools

The governors must first notify the local education authority in writing of the vacancy. Where there is going to be a gap between permanent appointments, the governors are free to make an appointment as acting head or acting deputy. The LEA will confirm the appointment subject to staff qualification requirements — defined as eligibility to teach, health and physical capacity/fitness or educational or other grounds. Should the LEA decline to confirm an acting headship or deputy headship appointment, the governors then recommend another person for the appointment.

All permanent posts as head or deputy head must be advertised nationally by the governors. Applications are considered by a selection panel of at least three governors which will short-list and then interview candidates. The panel recommends one of the candidates for approval by the full governing body. Following that approval, the governors recommend the candidate to the LEA which will confirm the appointment, subject to staff qualification requirements.

If the selection panel is unable to agree or the governing body declines to approve the panel's recommendation, the governors may require the selection panel to reconsider the candidates, following a further advertisement if governors so decide. The same procedure would be followed if the LEA should decline to confirm an appointment recommended by the governors.

The Chief Education Officer (or his representative) is entitled to attend all meetings of the governing body or selection panel where the appointment (including an acting appointment) of a head teacher or deputy head teacher is being considered. The Chief Education Officer (or his representative) must offer any appropriate advice which must be considered by the governors before they take their decision. For deputy head appointments the head teacher enjoys exactly the same rights as the Chief Education Officer.

Appointment of assistant teachers to county, controlled and special schools

It is open to governors to delegate any or all of their responsibilities in the appointment of assistant teachers to one or more governors, to the head alone or to the head acting together with one or more governors. Where the appointment is to be for four months or less, governors have complete freedom to recommend an appointment, subject to the LEA's confirmation of staff qualification requirements.

For all other teaching vacancies the governors must decide a job specification for the post and send a copy to the LEA. The LEA can propose for appointment to the post any current or potential employee of the LEA or, subject to their agreement, of voluntary aided governors, who seems to be qualified to fill a vacancy. Unless the governors decide to appoint to the post a person nominated by the LEA or a member of the school's current staff the post is then advertised externally, in such a way as to bring it to the attention of qualified applicants.

Governors can interview any candidates (including any which were proposed by the LEA) and recommend an appointment to the LEA which will then confirm subject to staff qualification requirements. If, following interview, the governors should decide to accept a candidate nominated by the LEA that appointment will be confirmed automatically. Should the LEA decline to confirm the governors' recommendation the governors reconsider the matter, conducting further interviews and readvertising if they wish to do so.

The Chief Education Officer (or his representative) is entitled to attend any proceedings which relate to the appointment of an assistant teacher. At governors' request the Chief Education Officer (or his representative) must offer any appropriate advice which governors are then required to consider prior to their decision. The head teacher enjoys exactly the same advisory rights as the Chief Education Officer.

References

When making appointments, governors need reliable information about the performance of the applicant in the current post.

This may be a reference from another authority or school, a report from an adviser on behalf of the Chief Education Officer about an applicant from within the authority, or a report from a college or department of education concerning a new entrant to the profession. In most cases, these references are sent as confidential documents and governors should take care to ensure that they are treated with the utmost discretion. It is normal convention that confidential reports are not photocopied but are retained by the chairman and read to fellow interviewers during the selection process.

Role of advisers

The adviser, or inspector as many authorities describe him, is a member of the Chief Education Officer's staff who plays a vital role in sustaining, developing and improving the quality of the education service throughout the authority. The advisory team is charged with monitoring and evaluating the performance of schools and of individual teachers, and with seeking to initiate and support educational developments. They have a particularly important role in the selection, training and development of staff. Many specialist advisers carry, in addition, general responsibilities and will be attached to individual schools or areas of the authority in order to provide general and pastoral support to heads and their staff.

Governors should always ensure that the fullest use is made of advice from the authority's advisers or education officers when making staff appointments. This specialist advice from outside the school is particularly helpful in providing a bench mark of quality for governors and for ensuring that their choice is informed by current best practice.

Induction of new staff

All new appointees, however experienced, will benefit from support and encouragement, especially during their early days at the school. Although a formal probationary period for newly-qualified teachers is to be abolished from 1992, this will not remove the need for a planned programme of professional induction. The first year of teaching is particularly demanding and newly-qualified teachers will require particular support both profes-

sionally and personally. Senior staff, governors and the LEA share
a responsibility for the professional welcome given to entrants
to teaching — they are much too valuable a resource to be allowed to become dispirited or overwhelmed by their first post.

A certain amount of teacher turnover is no bad thing for any
school since it enables fresh ideas and interests to inform the
school's work. On the other hand, rapid staff turnover can
be very harmful to educational quality within the school and
probably reveals some shortcomings in staff management. The
retention of skilled and motivated staff is just as important as
their appointment.

Salaries

Governors of schools with delegated budgets are responsible
for awarding any discretionary payments to heads and teachers
over and above their legal entitlement. Clearly, this is one of
the most sensitive areas in which governors will be asked to
reach decisions and it is one over which great care needs to be
exercised.

The criteria for the award of discretionary payments will
be set out in the current Pay and Conditions Document
and most authorities will supplement this with local advice.
The responsibility, however, is for the governors who must
ensure that decisions are financially prudent and meet the legal
conditions. Decision taking is improved if governors are able
to consider individual cases against an agreed school policy for
salaries. Certainly governors should apply consistent criteria
and should always be aware of the potential of their decision
for perceived unfairness or claims for comparability.

It is sound practice to delegate to a sub-committee individual
decisions within an agreed policy framework. This should
ensure that detailed consideration is given and that governors
uninvolved in the decision are available to consider any appeal
or grievance which might result.

Appraisal

A national scheme for the appraisal of all teachers (except
temporary and certain part-time teachers) was introduced in
September 1991, to be phased in over four years. Appraisal

is a positive exercise intended to further the development of teachers. Although the appraising body for all maintained schools is the LEA, the governors also have a key role to play in this important aspect of school life. It is the duty of the governors to see that the school complies with the appraisal regulations and that co-operation is extended to the LEA. Governors will need to satisfy themselves by regular reports from the head that appraisal is operating properly and to the benefit of the school. Governors may well be asked to approve expenditure arising from development needs identified during appraisal.

Governors can play a valuable part in the appraisal of the head. Governors will appoint one of the two appraisers for the heads of voluntary aided schools and for all schools the views of the chairman of governors should be consulted (with the full knowledge of the head) by those undertaking the appraisal. The chairman of governors will receive a copy of the head's completed appraisal — this information must be kept strictly confidential and should be used positively to support the head personally and professionally. The chairman can also request from the head any targets which have been agreed for particular teachers — again these will be confidential documents to be used in positive support of the teacher.

Staff discipline

Governors have responsibility for establishing and implementing staff discipline and grievance procedures which must be made known to the staff. The LEA is required to comply with governors' decisions relating to staff discipline. In cases of suspected or alleged misconduct, it is possible for the governors or the head teacher to suspend (on full pay) anyone who works at the school where that person's exclusion is considered necessary. It should be noted that suspension is a neutral act which does not imply any wrongdoing but simply affords an opportunity for matters to be investigated rationally and calmly. Whichever party suspends a member of staff must immediately inform the other party and the LEA. Only the governors may end a suspension, at which time the head teacher and the LEA must be informed immediately.

In extreme cases governors have the power to decide that someone (except school meals staff funded centrally) employed to work at the school should no longer work there. The LEA must be informed in writing with reasons for the governors' decision. Where that person is employed solely at the school and does not resign, the LEA must within 14 days give notice of dismissal (unless the circumstances justify summary dismissal). Where the person is not employed solely at the school, the LEA must withdraw him from work there.

Before a decision is taken to dismiss a member of staff, an opportunity must be provided for the person to make representations to the governors or their nominee(s). Before a dismissal decision is notified to the LEA, the person must have had an opportunity of making an appeal.

The Chief Education Officer (or his representative) and the head teacher (unless he is the subject of the action) are entitled to attend all proceedings in order to give advice which must be considered before a decision is reached.

These represent, of course, only the basic legal steps and most authorities will have recommended much fuller disciplinary and appeal procedures for adoption by their governors. It is absolutely essential that any disciplinary proceedings should be carried out with scrupulous attention to procedural propriety and to the rules of natural justice. Governors are strongly advised to consult established procedures and to seek specialist advice at the very earliest stages of any disciplinary proceedings.

In the case of voluntary aided schools, where the governors are the employers, the Chief Education Officer (or his representative) is involved only to the extent that the governors have decided to accord him advisory rights over appointment and/or dismissal of teachers. Where advisory rights have been given to the Chief Education Officer, he will be entitled to attend all relevant proceedings of the governing body (including interviews) for the purpose of giving advice. The Secretary of State has a reserve power to give those advisory rights to a Chief Education Officer where he considers it appropriate.

Redundancy

As the governors can now determine the number of staff to be deployed at a school, they may also determine when that number must be reduced. Employees have the right not to be dismissed unfairly and it is crucial that governors should follow exactly procedures which will be fair and in accordance with employment law. Most education authorities will have a recommended procedure, usually agreed with the recognised professional associations, which will encompass all the necessary safeguards. Unless governors are the employers of the staff, they will not themselves be involved in the issue of redundancy documents. However, now that education authorities have no powers to redeploy staff from one school to another (except by the agreement of the receiving governing body) a decision to require the withdrawal of an employee may be tantamount to deciding that person's redundancy. This simply reinforces the need for the greatest care and fairness should it be necessary to reduce the staffing establishment in this way.

It is important that governors investigate all feasible options before looking to require the removal of a member of staff. Such options will usually include what is inelegantly called 'natural wastage' — i.e. staff taking retirement or posts elsewhere. In addition, it may be possible to make the necessary staffing reduction by voluntary agreement, perhaps by job share or reduced part-time hours.

There can be no other area of governors' responsibilities which is so sensitive, both within the school and in relations with parents and the wider community. Not surprisingly, teacher opinion about a school will often owe much to the way in which the vital issues of employment have been tackled by the governors. It is essential that everyone concerned should be confident that clear and fair criteria have been applied consistently and sympathetically.

Early retirement in the interest of the service

As pupil numbers in primary and secondary schools gradually fell in the 1970s and 1980s, education authorities increasingly managed the contraction of the service by facilitating the early retirement of teachers. With pupil numbers now showing an increase and with a shortage of teachers in particular areas, early retirement may become a less common strategy. Moreover, with delegated budgets the cost of financing early retirement with enhanced pension is shifting from central budgets to individual school budgets which may find it more difficult to identify the necessary initial funding. It is likely, however, that early retirement will remain one of the ways of achieving 'natural wastage'. The precise details of the schemes will vary across authorities but, in essence, the principle is that a teacher aged 50 years, with five or more years' service, may be retired if the employer agrees, with or without enhanced pension (i.e. pension increased as if the teacher had accomplished more than his actual years of service). This enhancement may not exceed the shortest of the following periods:

(a)   a period of 10 years
(b)   a period equivalent in length to the teacher's eligible service
(c)   a period such as to make the teacher's eligible service not exceed 40 years
(d)   a period up to the date when the teacher reaches 65 years of age.

Sometimes, the pension enhancement may be linked to re-dundancy payments where the teacher's post is not being replaced.

Governors should note that in county, voluntary controlled and special agreement schools the authority must certify that the early retirement is in the interests of 'the more efficient exercise of the authority's function'. In voluntary aided schools, the governors are the employers of the teachers and the governors may, therefore, take the initiative in a case of early retirement. It is the LEA, however, which must certify to the DES that the teacher is leaving pensionable service in accordance with the provisions for early retirement.

Employment legislation

As mentioned above, this legislation is complex and subject to changing interpretation because of the great body of case law. Authorities will employ, or have access to, specialists in this field and may well have produced handbooks of guidance for governors.

The key pieces of legislation are:

1.   *Employment Protection Consolidation Act 1978:* this provides that an employee must have a written statement of terms and conditions of employment and, after 104 weeks' service, have the right not to be unfairly dismissed. If an employee considers he has been unfairly dismissed, he has access to an industrial tribunal which can award him compensation or make an order for reinstatement or re-engagement.
     The dismissal of an employee may be found to be

unfair if it has not been preceded by a sequence of events designed to warn him and offer him help and guidance over a reasonable period before deciding to dismiss.

The local education authority, will, no doubt, have laid down procedures which conform to the requirements of this Act. Failure to observe the essential requirements could lead to very damaging results, including the possible reinstatement of an unsatisfactory teacher or the payment of considerable sums in compensation. Governors acting in close consultation with the Chief Education Officer and in accordance with the recommended procedures are unlikely to find themselves in this difficulty.

2. *Race Relations Act 1976:* the Race Relations legislation is intended to make discrimination in employment on grounds of race unlawful. An appointing body must be quite sure that its reasons for preferring one candidate to another do not include any element of discrimination and are such as can be defended. An aggrieved person has access to the Commission for Racial Equality. It is important to note that discrimination may be direct or indirect — i.e. applying conditions which effectively rule out applicants from particular racial backgrounds.

Equally, governors will need to take the same care in their dealings with those who are already on the school staff. The exercise of governor powers over promotion or staff discipline needs to be above any suggestion of personal favour or disadvantage.

3. *Sex Discrimination Act 1975:* equal opportunities legislation is intended to prevent discrimination in employment caused by the unequal treatment of men and women. An appointing body must check its advertisements to ensure that there is no suggestion that either men or women are specifically excluded from consideration. If a person feels that he or she has been discriminated against, a complaint may be taken first to the Equal Opportunities Commission (EOC) or to a industrial tribunal and then to the county court if it appears that the complainant's sex has been taken into account in making an appointment or an award or a dismissal.

Again, this is an area where early consultation and a readiness to listen to specialist advice will be of invaluable assistance to governors.

Conditions of service

The main duties of teachers are contained in the Pay and Conditions Document (Appendix A). However, there are many aspects of teachers' conditions of service which rest on agreements which have been negotiated between the associations of local authorities and the recognised teachers' associations. There will be local variations in each authority but the following headings may be of particular interest to governors:

1. *Maternity leave:* A female employee is entitled, subject to qualifying service, to paid maternity leave and has the right to return to work. The employee must give not less than 14 weeks' notice of her confinement and should notify her employer at least 21 days before her absence begins. If she wishes to return to work, she must do so not later than 29 weeks after her confinement and give at least one week's notice of her return. Any absence beyond the 29 weeks must be covered by a medical certificate.

    Some authorities have also introduced arrangements for paternity leave.

2. *Leave for public duties:* National conditions of service allow teachers to have paid leave for certain public duties, e.g. Justice of the Peace, membership of local or public authorities, military reserve. The LEA will either have embodied these in its own agreement with the teachers' associations or have a separate arrangement.

3. *Trade union leave:* teachers and other staff have a right to leave of absence under agreed conditions for trade union activities. The authority will have negotiated facilities for trade union representatives, with the cost of any agreed absence usually falling to central funds rather than to school budgets.

4. *Grievance procedure:* it is required under the 1988 Education Reform Act that governors should establish their own grievance procedures for staff. As with disciplinary procedures, most authorities will have offered to governors a recommended grievance procedure which will satisfy both legal and practical requirements. Suitable adjustments will need to be made to recognise the separate character of voluntary aided schools. Sensitive application of sound grievance procedures may nip in the bud many potentially damaging disputes and so save time, goodwill and reputation.

5. *Special leave:* the local education authority will have its own regulations specifying the circumstances under

which special leave may be granted and the method of granting it. Local schemes will often give a certain amount of discretion to governors and heads to grant leave in circumstances falling outside the normal provisions.

Support staff

These include school secretaries, administrative and clerical assistants, laboratory and workshop technicians, librarians, school meals staff, welfare assistants, nursery nurses, caretakers and groundsmen.

In county and controlled schools the support staff are employed by the local authority. In voluntary aided schools they are employed, except for school meals staff, by the governors, usually in accordance with terms and conditions laid down by the local authority.

These staff have exactly the same rights under the Employment Protection and Consolidation Act, Race Relations Act and Sex Discrimination Act as teachers and their appointment, conditions and dismissal are subject to the same legal conditions and constraints. The procedures for appointment and dismissal for support staff (except school meals staff) are detailed in the 1988 Education Reform Act. Governors have the power to delegate the power of appointment to one or more governors, to the head alone or to the head acting together with one or more governors. Before an appointment is recommended to the LEA, consultation must have taken place with the head and (for posts of 16 hours per week or more) the Chief Education Officer. When a candidate has been selected the LEA must be notified in writing of the recommended appointment, detailing the hours of work and grade of appointment. The LEA will then implement the recommendation subject to staff qualification requirements.

In practice, it is likely that the majority of support staff appointments will be made by the head teacher, sometimes accompanied by a specialist member of the Chief Education Officer's staff.

Conditions of service

These are negotiated nationally between representatives of local authorities and the trade unions. There are separate agreements for officers (secretaries, clerical staff, technicians and nurses) and for manual workers. These national agreements are supplemented by provincial and local agreements.

1. *Period of notice:* the notice to be given to the employer will normally be one week or one month depending on the contract and type of employee. The notice given to an employee depends upon the period of continuous service. The maximum period of notice is 12 weeks.

2. *Probationary service:* all new employees will serve a six month probationary period during which their suitability for continued employment is assessed.

3. *Sickness regulations:* these will form part of the contract and conditions of service.

4. *Annual and public holidays:* support staff are entitled variously to paid annual and public holidays in accordance with their conditions of service. Support staff in schools are normally required to take annual holidays during the closure periods.

5. *Special leave:* support staff may be granted special leave on compassionate grounds for cases of bereavement and close family illness.

6. *Disciplinary procedure:* as for teachers, governors are responsible for drawing up and implementing disciplinary procedures. Support staff also have the right to make representations before any decision to dismiss and to appeal against such a decision before it is implemented by the local education authority.

There must also be a grievance procedure for support staff. Many authorities have recommended to governors procedures which are applicable for all staff in the school, whatever their role.

The need for sensitivity and concern for natural justice is just as crucial with support staff as it is with teachers.

LEA support staff

The local education authority will support the work of schools through a variety of support staff. Contact with these staff is normally through the head teacher. The governors should be aware of the extent of specialist support available.

Advisers/Inspectors provide specialist management and curriculum advice to schools and to the Chief Education Officer and Education Committee.

Education welfare officers are concerned with school attendance and with the circumstances of the child and his family which may affect attendance. Their information is an invaluable supplement to the school's knowledge of a child. With the introduction of Education Supervision Orders under the Children Act 1989 the role of the Education Welfare Officer can be of even greater assistance to schools.

Educational psychologists are usually on the staff of the Chief Education Officer. They work in schools and in individual consultation with teachers, children and parents. They advise on educational and behavioural difficulties. In addition, they help to assess children with special educational needs.

Consultant psychiatrists are employed by the local health authority and will work with disturbed children.

Community medical officers are employed by the local health authority. In addition to medical inspections of children, they will advise on any problems of school health faced by schools, e.g. outbreaks of infectious disease.

Dental officers are employed by the local health authority and they inspect, treat and advise in their own field.

Social workers are employed by the Social Services Committee of the local authority and may be in contact with a school about a child or family they are helping. Schools are seen as crucial contacts for social workers.

Speech therapists and physiotherapists are normally employed by the health authority to provide specialist support to children in pre-school, mainstream and special establishments.

10
Children with special educational needs

The Warnock Report on *The Education of Handicapped Children and Young People* (1978) suggested that about 20% of all children will at some point in their school lives experience significant learning difficulties. That is, they will have a degree of special educational needs which will require particular consideration, beyond that required by the majority of children, if they are to obtain the maximum benefit from their education and to develop their full potential.

Within that group there will be a smaller number, around 2% of all children, whose learning difficulties and special needs are so great that they are likely to require specific protection and procedures to ensure that their needs are met.

Children with special educational needs, by these definitions, will be found in mainstream schools, in special units and centres attached to mainstream schools, in special schools and in independent schools specifically provided for special needs. However, it is important to remember that all children have individual needs and that, within every local authority and each school, provision must be planned to ensure that all children have a full range of educational opportunities in which they can develop their full potential.

Definitions

The 1981 Education Act defines a child as having special educational needs requiring special educational provision if he has:

either   a significantly greater difficulty in learning than the majority of children of his age

or   a disability which either prevents or hinders him from making use of educational facilities of a kind generally provided in schools . . . . . . for children of his age *or*   is under the age of five and is in one of these categories or is likely to be so later if special educational provision is not made.

Special education provision is defined as:

educational provision which is additional to, or otherwise different from, the educational provision made generally for children of his age in schools . . . .

The 1981 Education Act further provides that where an authority has decided that special educational provision is to be arranged for a child, it is the duty of the authority to make that provision in an ordinary school (after taking account of the parents' views) as long as this is compatible with:

(a)   the child receiving the special educational provision that he requires;

(b)   the provision of efficient education for the other children with whom he will be educated;

(c)   the efficient use of resources.

These provisions are important both for local authorities and for governors considering integration of children with special needs in mainstream schools.

Procedures

The 1981 Education Act greatly extended the rights and involvement of parents in the assessment and provision for children with special needs. The DES in its guidance on the 1981 Act stressed the concept of partnership not only with parents but also with older children and young people with special needs and urged that the feelings and perceptions of the child concerned should be taken into account.

These principles are clearly carried into the duties and procedures required of local education authorities in the formal assessment and statementing of children for whom special educational provision is likely to be required, that is, those children who may fall within the 2% set out in the Warnock Report and identified in the 1981 Education Act.

Where there is a *prima facie* case for considering that a child has special educational needs, the local authority must inform the parents of the proposal to carry out a formal assessment of the child's needs. The parents have a right of comment or objection, to submit their views and to be involved in the assessment and advice provided by medical and educational psychology staff. When the authority produces its statement of special educational needs, that is the summary of the child's needs and the intended provision accompanied by copies of all the professional advice, the parents have the right to comment on the draft and to appeal, if they are dissatisfied, against the final version. If they are dissatisfied with the outcome of the local independent appeal committee hearing, parents may take their appeal to the Secretary of State. Once a statement has been issued, there must be annual reviews to consider whether the child's special needs have changed and whether provision to meet those needs should be changed. Again, there are clear rights of parental representation if the LEA proposes to alter the statement or to cease to maintain a statement on the child.

As well as assessment in individual cases, the local authority must keep under review its whole range of special educational provision and ensure that an appropriate range of provision is available.

Governors' responsibilities

The 1981 Education Act placed particular responsibilities on school governors in respect of special educational needs:

(a) to use their best endeavours, in exercising their functions in relation to the school, to secure that if any registered pupil has special educational needs, the special educational provision that is required for him is made;

(b) to secure that, where the responsible person has been informed by the local education authority that a registered pupil has special educational needs, those needs are made known to all who are likely to teach him;

(c) to secure that the teachers in the school are aware of the importance of identifying, and providing for, those registered pupils who have special educational needs.

In this context, the 'responsible person' may be the chairman of governors, another designated governor, or the head teacher.

There is also a requirement that where a child with special educational needs is admitted to an ordinary school, steps must be taken to ensure that the child engages in the activities of the school with the other children who do not have special educational needs.

Other considerations

The 1988 Education Reform Act has further particular implications for children with special educational needs. The National Curriculum applies to both mainstream and special schools and to all pupils. Children with special educational needs will be expected to have full access to the National Curriculum and to the associated requirements for pupil assessment, programmes of study and attainment targets, unless clearly specified procedures are invoked. A statement of special educational needs may modify or disapply any or all of the requirements of the National Curriculum for an individual pupil if they are inappropriate in that case. Where a pupil does not have a statement, the head teacher may modify or disapply the requirements of the National Curriculum for limited periods. These provisions contain careful safeguards and parents may appeal.

The introduction of LMS has raised major issues about special needs provision in mainstream schools. Traditionally, many local authorities have held centrally the additional special needs funds to be provided for statemented and non-statemented children in schools as well as the costs of special educational needs support and assessment staff. Decisions are now required on the extent to which these funds should be devolved. Many authorities are devolving a part of the funds, for non-statemented children, while retaining funds to give effect to statements and to pay support staff, including educational psychologists, but this is an area where further change may occur. By 1994 formula funding (and possibly delegated management) is to be extended to special schools.

With all these changes, the local authority remains responsible for assessment and statements, giving effect to statements through appropriate provision and admission of children to mainstream as well as special schools.

Continuing concerns

Although the 1981 Education Act was a great milestone in recognising and providing for special educational needs, its implementation has not always been smooth or without controversy, and major concerns remain:

1. A great many children have been identified as having special educational needs requiring additional provision

but the requirement for additional resources properly to meet those needs has placed an enormous strain on local authority budgets.

2. The statutory procedures have proved very expensive in staff time and can be lengthy and bureaucratic; while protecting the rights of the individual, they can also give rise to extensive disputes and litigation.

3. Integration, in its fullest sense, has been patchy; special schools have declined in number as much because of declining pupil numbers as because of policies of integration, and those which remain are in many cases small with consequent problems in finance and organisation.

4. The demands on teaching and support staff in meeting special educational needs are great and raise profound issues for initial training, in-service training and development of skills; there are serious skill shortages, for example speech therapists.

5. The pressures of LMS, More Open Enrolment and the National Curriculum may pose particular challenges in ensuring that children with special educational needs receive appropriate provision.

An agenda for governors

The challenges for governors of meeting special educational needs responsibilities are very great. Governors should as far as possible:

1. Ascertain and understand basic special needs procedures and the arrangements which apply in their local authority and school.

2. Ensure that there is a whole school policy for meeting individual pupil needs and, within that, flexible arrangements for identifying and meeting special educational needs, including the needs of the most able.

3. Ensure that special educational needs are fully and equitably considered in school organisation, budget deployment, staffing priorities, development and training, particularly in the context of LMS.

4. Consider appointing a governor to take a particular interest in special educational needs.

5. Ensure that special educational needs are a regular feature of reports which they receive.

6.   Seek training opportunities which include special educational needs and consider inviting specialists, such as officers, inspectors and educational psychologists, to address their meetings.

7.   Ensure that links with parents and the community make sensitive and constructive references to special educational needs.

8.   Ensure that children with special educational needs are given particular consideration in careers and vocational guidance as they approach their leaving date.

The responsibilities of a governor in a special school are not fundamentally different from those in a mainstream school. By definition, special schools provide for children with special educational needs. Special schools may provide for a particular type of need: moderate learning difficulties, severe learning difficulties, physical handicap, sensory impairment (sight, hearing, language), emotional and behavioural difficulties, or may provide, on an area basis, for a range of moderate difficulties. In some cases there will be boarding provision, raising issues of care outside the school day.

Governors of a special school will need a deeper understanding of special educational needs, procedures and provisions, and the links with parents and the community may be more demanding, but also, potentially, very rewarding. Good liaison with Health and Social Services Departments and voluntary bodies will be particularly important. The presence on special school governing bodies of appointees from the voluntary sector should be of particular value here. The appropriate application of the National Curriculum will be another major concern for governors. The introduction of LMS to special schools will require particular care to ensure that the needs of the individual child on the one hand, and the place of the special school in the local authority's range of provision on the other, are both safeguarded.

11
Discipline and exclusion of pupils

Discipline and support

Each school needs a disciplinary structure for pupils which will provide support, guidance and security for them as well as control and order for the school. The governors, in their responsibility for the general direction of the conduct of the school, may set out certain general principles for the head teacher and guidance in relation to particular matters of discipline. Thereafter, the head is required to determine and implement the measures necessary to promote among pupils self-discipline, proper regard for authority, and good and acceptable standards of behaviour. The local education authority must be consulted in advance over any proposed measures which might lead to increased expenditure or affect its responsibilities as an employer. (In extreme cases where discipline has broken down, the local education authority, following written advice to the governing body, has a reserve power to assume direct control of a county, controlled or special school and to give directions to the governors and head. Governors and heads of aided and special agreement schools in such circumstances cannot be directed by the LEA but must consider any representation from the LEA.)

There needs to be a clear and sympathetic understanding between the head, staff and governors over the disciplinary structure and its purpose, and their understanding should also include parents and pupils. The relationship between the teacher and the pupils is significantly different from that of a generation ago. Particularly at secondary level, there is a more explicit emphasis on partnership in the learning process, and that partnership will best be promoted within an atmosphere of mutual respect.

Corporal punishment in maintained schools was abolished in 1987. The 1986 Education Act made it clear that legally no teacher could claim a right to use corporal punishment by virtue of his office (except to avert an immediate danger of personal injury or danger to property). In the wake of this change, many local education authorities will have reviewed their disciplinary practices and the alternative courses of action. The governing body, representing the local community as well as parents and teachers, is in an ideal position to discuss, design and review a school's policy in this respect.

Ideally, effective discipline will emerge naturally from a positive attitude towards good behaviour and an atmosphere within the school of constructive, purposeful activity. Expectations may well have a part to play in determining pupils' behaviour but, even more important, will be the example set by teachers and parents. Schools cannot act on their own. Young people are subject to many influences and predominant amongst these will be the influence of the home. It is vitally important that schools and parents co-operate in relation to behaviour. The disciplinary demands of school and home are bound to differ. Schools will need to tell parents about their policies; and to be effective, both school and home need to be consistent in the way in which they exercise their own discipline.

Exclusion

In the face of extreme misbehaviour and unsuccessful mediation, the legal sanction available to schools is the exclusion of pupils. Clearly, exclusion is to be regarded as a last resort and schools will generally go to great lengths before deciding that a child has to be removed. The statutory procedures and appeal arrangements are detailed in Sections 23–27 of the 1986 Education Act. They embody the shared responsibility carried by the head, the governors and the LEA and in the most serious cases they also ensure a hearing for parental views. It is significant that when the procedures have run their course the ultimate authority is always vested in the governors.

Given the interdependence of the various interests and the inherent sensitivity of the issue it is not surprising that the procedures are somewhat complex. The following summary highlights the key points:

1. *General*
    (a) Exclusion relates to action taken on disciplinary grounds (and not, for example, health reasons).
    (b) Only a head has the power to exclude a pupil from attendance.

(c)   Parents act for pupils below the age of 18 — pupils of 18 and over act for themselves.
(d)   There are three types of exclusion — temporary, indefinite and permanent — and procedures will vary according to the type of exclusion.

2. *Temporary exclusions*

(a)   Parents are informed by the head of the exclusion, its duration and cause. They are also told of their right to make representations to the governors and LEA.
(b)   The governors and LEA must be informed by the head where a temporary exclusion will lead to the pupil's absence for more than five days (in aggregate) in any one term or to the loss of an opportunity to take a public examination. In such cases the head must comply with any direction for reinstatement issued by the governors or LEA (who must inform each other and the parent of any such direction).
(c)   Before giving any direction for reinstatement, the LEA must have consulted the governors.
(d)   Where conflicting directions have been received from the governors and LEA, the head must comply with the one that would lead to the pupil's earlier reinstatement.

3. *Indefinite exclusions*

(a)   This type of exclusion may arise where a temporary exclusion has not produced the desired outcome or where reports are required to inform a decision about the pupil's future.
(b)   Parents are informed by the head of the exclusion and the reasons for it. They are also told of their right to make representations to the governors and the LEA.
(c)   The governors and LEA must be informed by the head of all indefinite exclusions. The LEA is then under a duty to consult the governors concerning the indefinite exclusion. Where the governors either do not intend to direct the pupil's reinstatement or (in the LEA's view) set an unreasonable date for a reinstatement, the LEA must issue directions to the head for the pupil's reinstatement either immediately or at a set time.
(d)   It is the duty of the head to comply with such a direction unless he should then decide that the pupil's exclusion should be made permanent.

4. *Permanent exclusions (or expulsions)*

(a) The routes to this ultimate sanction may be by the head making permanent what began as a temporary or indefinite exclusion or (in extreme cases) by the immediate imposition of permanent exclusion. In either case the head must immediately inform the parents, the governors and the LEA, giving reasons for the decision.

(b) The LEA is under a duty to consult the governors and decide whether the pupil should be reinstated either immediately or at a particular date or not at all.

(c) Where the LEA considers that the pupil should be reinstated, it must give the appropriate direction to the head. Where reinstatement is not being pursued, the LEA must notify the parent of the decision.

(d) This is the point at which the statutory appeal procedures come into play. The LEA must make arrangements for the hearing of appeals from:

(i) parents of pupils whom the LEA does not intend to reinstate or

(ii) governors of schools being directed to reinstate a permanently excluded pupil.

(e) The detailed arrangements for the conduct of appeals are set out in Schedule 3 of the 1986 Education Act. The critical factors are:

(i) Any LEA direction for reinstatement will not have effect for seven days, during which time the governors can notify the LEA of their intention to appeal (or not). A contested reinstatement will not be implemented pending the outcome of the appeal procedure.

(ii) The composition of the appeal committee is for the LEA to determine but it must be constituted as for the hearing of school admission appeals under the 1980 Education Act.

(iii) Appeals are to be in writing and appellants have the right to attend and to be represented.

NOTE: These appeal arrangements relating to permanent exclusions are mandatory. There is also a discretionary power for LEAs to include in the Articles of Government rights of appeal in cases of temporary or indefinite exclusion.

5. *Arrangements in voluntary aided and special agreement schools*
With one significant exception, the legal procedures in these

schools are the same as described above. The exception concerns appeals against permanent exclusion where only the governors have the power to direct the reinstatement of a pupil.

General considerations

The 1986 legislation aimed to overcome the uncertainty over the legal position of the respective partners, and to avoid problems which had arisen where direction for a pupil's reinstatement by the LEA had led to a refusal by teachers to accept that pupil into their classes. Since then, similar problems have arisen from reinstatements directed by a school's governors. This simply goes to show that problems with individual pupils are bound to occur, and tolerance and close consultation will always be required on the part of the LEA, governors, teachers and parents if the position is to be resolved satisfactorily, with the needs of other pupils also taken into account.

Most authorities will have devised, in consultation with their heads and teachers, general codes of practice for the exclusion of pupils and will have set out the range of alternative options that might be available if a return to the same school is not considered appropriate. Authorities will almost certainly have available a variety of support services, including sometimes special centres, for those pupils whose behaviour is likely to lead to, or has resulted in, exclusion. Governors should be aware of the nature and scale of this alternative provision.

Experience has shown that many of the worst disciplinary problems could have been avoided, or at least minimised, if there had been earlier and closer contact between the school and the parents over the pupil's problems. Heads should give their governors regular reports on disciplinary matters, and, in particular, on any exclusions. Heads may sometimes find it helpful to have the support of the chairman or another member of the governing body when discussing with the parents persistent behavioural problems and how to prevent them recurring. Sometimes parents may have been quite unaware of the child's difficulties and find that such a meeting suffices to alert them to the need for action to redress the position. At the other extreme, it may emerge through such a meeting that the parents may be quite unable to cope and support for the family is urgently required from specialist agencies.

The circumstances are infinitely variable, and each case requires sympathetic and individual handling. The governors will, rightly, be interested in the outcome of each case for its bearing on their fundamental responsibility for the conduct of the school. Many experienced observers regard a school's approach and actions in this difficult area as one of the key indicators of its real values and priorities.

12
Provision of schools, premises and grounds

There are three major aspects of the responsibility for provision of schools and for their premises and grounds:

1. Provision of schools, opening, closing and altering schools.
2. Repair, maintenance and upkeep.
3. Control and use of premises.

In both county and voluntary schools, responsibility in each of these aspects is shared between the providers of the school and its premises, (the local education authority or the trustees), and the governors. The fine details of how that responsibility is shared are a very complicated matter and are set out very fully in *County and Voluntary Schools* (7th Edition 1989). There may also be variation from one local authority to another in responsibilities for premises and it is important that governors should be familiar with the Articles of Government and Local Management of Schools Scheme referring to their school. This chapter sets out the general position.

County schools
Provision of schools, opening, closing and altering schools

These are, first, matters of legal procedure and the relevant provisions are found mostly in the 1944 and 1980 Education Acts. A local education authority has a duty to ensure that there are sufficient schools for its area and to provide those schools according to its overall policy. This may involve the following processes:

1. *Opening a New School:* in an area of housing or population growth, to replace an old school, or (rarely) to maintain as a county school one which was previously voluntary.

2. *Closing a school:* where the number of pupils is felt to be too low to justify retaining a school or allow it to be viable (this can occur in both urban and rural settings), or where the building is outworn. The LEA may also propose to cease to fund a voluntary school.

Closing a school and opening a new school (sometimes in the same premises) can be the means of effecting a major change in organisation, for example from grammar/secondary modern to comprehensive.

3. *Significant change of character:* this is a technical term embracing such changes as selective to comprehensive admissions, single sex admissions to mixed, or a change of age range, for example, middle to secondary.

4. *Significant enlargement:* this is where it is proposed to increase significantly the number of pupils admitted, with additional buildings (and is thus different from an increase in the standard number for admissions within existing premises).

There is no specific legal procedure for amalgamating two schools. Either, both must close and a new school be opened, or one school must be closed and the other enlarged and/or changed.

In all these procedures, the local education authority must reach a decision after consulting the governors, the parents and the community affected. A Public Notice must be issued for two months giving rights of objection and if there is objection or if the Secretary of State regards the matter as sufficiently important then the final decision rests with him. Once approved, the proposals must be implemented according to the proposed timetable.

Governors are involved in these matters in a number of important ways. In the case of a new school, the LEA must arrange for the appointment of a temporary governing body since the governing body is formally constituted only when a school opens. The temporary governing body will therefore be involved in a wide range of activities and preparations including staff appointments, staffing structure, financial planning and parental and community links. If there are to be new buildings or extension or modification of existing buildings there will be the opportunity to be consulted by the local authority in planning and design.

Closures of schools and significant changes can be controversial and hotly contested matters involving disagreement between the local authority and the community. The LEA may see pressing reasons for change within its overall responsibilities including demographic and economic arguments and concerns about admissions policies. The local community may, understandably, resist and stress concerns based on local issues, the immediate needs of the community, safety and avoiding longer journeys to school. The discussion of the future of a small community school is a classic instance of this dilemma.

Governors may well find themselves in the middle of such arguments and will need to balance the community concerns against the authority's case, but always bearing in mind the medium to long term educational interests of the children and ensuring that proper weight is given to these fundamental concerns. It is an exercise which requires mature judgement based on a wide understanding of the school and the community and the broader picture of overall educational provision.

These pressures have been increased by the advice from the Audit Commission to local authorities to take more surplus places out of use and the ability of schools to apply for grant maintained status so that they are no longer subject to local authority proposals.

New school premises and buildings

When new schools are opened, it is the duty of the local authority to finance and provide the site and the buildings. These must conform to the School Premises Regulations which cover such matters as the size of buildings, the range of facilities (to meet organisational and curriculum requirements) and the scale of recreational and sports areas.

Governors frequently ask why these Regulations do not apply to existing schools, especially if they lack facilities. It is widely acknowledged that enormous investment will be required to bring existing schools up to standard. The requirement to bring existing schools up to the standards of the School Premises

Regulations has been put back from 1991 to 1996 and there are serious doubts whether it will be achieved even by then.

Financing new premises and buildings and improving existing buildings

Local authorities finance these projects from a number of sources:

1. *Borrowing*: borrowing must be contained within an annual credit approval limit set by central government.
2. *Revenue*: there is no limit to the use of current revenue funds but spending must be contained within overall local authority expenditure which is subject to Government regulations.
3. *Receipts*: where an asset, such as a redundant building or piece of land, is sold by the local authority the receipts may be used to finance new projects, subject to overall government limits on such procedures.

It will readily be seen that local authorities are not entirely free agents in financing capital projects but are subject to government macro-economic policy in public finance. The government is, however, concerned about the enormous scale of outstanding debt on public buildings. Governors will want to ensure that they are familiar with the procedures in their local authority for agreeing the authority's capital programme and to ensure that the needs of their school are brought to the attention of the authority. They may have concerns about the adequacy of the existing buildings in size, especially if pupil numbers are rising, the range of facilities, not least for different activities or to meet new curriculum demands in science and technology, or the general condition of the buildings. These should be referred to the LEA although the authority may then have a difficult task in drawing up priorities within a limited capital programme against a substantial backlog of desirable projects.

Schools and governing bodies may finance their own new buildings and improvements. They will normally be subject to reasonable local authority requirements in building safety and design, since the authority remains the owner of the site and buildings and has responsibilities for overall provision. There are also likely to be financial checks to ensure reasonable prudence and because school borrowing or leasing for building projects may affect the authority's own capital programme under government regulations.

Repair, maintenance and upkeep of premises and grounds

The condition of school premises has often given rise to concern. While it is frequently and justifiably said that a good teacher and well motivated pupils can produce outstanding results in poor conditions, it is also true that premises in good condition are conducive to good education. To put it the other way, the process of education can be adversely affected by poor accommodation.

This is an area where the introduction of LMS is bringing about significant changes in procedures and responsibilities. An analogy which is now frequently used is that the local authority is the 'landlord' and the school the 'tenant'. The local authority is the owner of the premises with ultimate responsibility for their upkeep and condition while schools are receiving greater devolved responsibility and freedom of action in considering their local priorities.

The details of such arrangements will vary from one authority to another. It is, therefore, essential that governors and head teachers are fully conversant with the articles of government and LMS scheme which apply to them. There may be other important provisions arising from the Health and Safety at Work Act (1974), the Local Government Act (1988) — competitive tendering — and LEA standing orders and financial regulations. The following is intended only as a general guide.

LMS schemes will include provisions setting out the respective responsibilities of LEA and governors in premises maintenance. Ideally these should include detailed schedules referring to the full range of items including the building structure, electrical, water and fuel services, internal and external maintenance and decoration, roads, playgrounds, grounds and fields, ancillary and temporary buildings, kitchens, heating plants, equipment and fire precautions.

In many authorities, the general division is that the LEA retains responsibility for major or structural items, basic electrical and mechanical services and major items of equipment, while the school has responsibility for the remainder.

It is very helpful if the authority produces a manual of guidance on premises issues. In any event, it is important to establish clear arrangements for liaison between school and authority on building work programmes (to avoid clashes or abortive works), provisions for emergency or out or school hours maintenance (on any items, regardless of general responsibility) and for responsibility and arrangements for servicing of important plant and equipment.

Governors need to establish procedures for considering buildings and premises matters and for financial planning to meet premises expenses. This is a question of responsibility but there may also be opportunities to direct funding into local priorities for improvements. Arrangements should also be made to consult with representatives of the local authority about items in their area of responsibility for maintenance.

Governors and heads will need to consider their responsibilities under the Health and Safety at Work Act for contributing to the health and safety of employees, pupils and visitors. The policy and guidelines of the LEA should be considered and school policies and staff responsibility clarified. The governors should consult the LEA about the position on indemnity insurance against claims arising from their alleged negligence.

Under the 1988 Local Government Act and other legislation, local authorities are required to submit certain services to competitive tendering including the cleaning of buildings and building and grounds maintenance. The general intention is that local authorities and schools should purchase services which will provide the best value for money, taking into account quality and convenience as well as price.

In many cases authorities have let tenders for the whole or part of their area for cleaning, grounds maintenance and response or other building maintenance. The LMS scheme should clarify the position and the dates of termination of such contracts, together with any remaining obligations on schools to use these contracts and the service specification. Following the termination of such contracts, governing bodies will be responsible for considering how to make arrangements for cleaning, grounds maintenance and building maintenance to the specification they require, whether by joining an authority-tendered scheme or otherwise. If a school organises its own direct service organisation then it must comply with the requirements of the Local Government Act 1988 on competitive tendering.

The governors should also clarify with the local authority the arrangements for insurance of premises and equipment including respective liabilities and the extent of any authority cover.

Control and use of premises

School buildings and grounds are valuable community assets. For many years it has been national policy to encourage joint use of premises by the school and other community groups. At one extreme, a school may be part of an extensive community complex including library, swimming pool, sports hall, drama and multi-purpose areas. At the other, a village primary school may have limited facilities but remain the only substantial local community building for meetings and activities.

The 1986 Education Act provides that 'governors shall have control of the school premises out of school hours, subject to any general direction by the local authority'. Such directions might include use of the school premises for adult education, the youth service or other LEA sponsored activities. Governors should be aware of any such local requirements.

Where there are joint use premises, governors should be clear on what constitutes the school premises under their control. For example, there may be special arrangements applying to a joint use sports hall or adjoining youth club or community centre with all the associated issues of access, parking, hours of use, financial and maintenance responsibilities and resolution of disputes.

LMS schemes have also had an impact on the letting of school premises. Governors will now generally receive the income from charges which they are free to set as long as they defray any expenditure involved. (Statutory lettings such as council meetings or elections may still involve a standard fee.) Governors should not create any tenancies or licences for long term use without the agreement and involvement of the LEA.

Sometimes, there can be delicate issues in letting school premises. Do school functions have priority over all community uses? Are some community uses incompatible with school needs? Governors will need to balance school and community considerations fairly but, in the end, the fundamental criterion is the operation of the school in the best interests of the pupils.

Voluntary schools

Under the 1980 Education Act, the governors of a voluntary aided or voluntary controlled school have very similar legal responsibilities for proposing the establishment of a new school or a significant change in an existing school as the local authority in respect of county schools.

The buildings, but not always the grounds, of a voluntary aided school will generally be owned by the trustees and the governors are responsible for major and external maintenance.

The local authority is generally responsible for internal maintenance and for certain specified areas including school meals accommodation, the caretaker's house, the medical room and buildings connected with the playing fields. The details are well set out in *County and Voluntary Schools* but governors of aided schools should in any event be clear about their liabilities, liaison with the local authority where responsibilities may overlap, emergency arrangements and the effects of the LMS scheme.

Governors of voluntary aided schools are responsible for financing new or improved buildings but may apply to central government for grant aid of up to 85%. They must also consult the local education authority which draws up the aided school capital building programme for its area and may have ongoing financial responsibilities from such schemes.

Most of what has been said about premises and buildings issues in county schools applies also to voluntary controlled schools. An exception is that the 1944 Education Act gives to the governors of voluntary controlled schools the control of the use of the school premises on Saturdays (unless a local authority direction is given concerning use for education or welfare purposes), and to the foundation governors the use of the school premises on Sundays.

Control of the school premises in voluntary aided and special agreement schools is in the hands of the governors.

13
Grant maintained schools

Although this book has been written principally to provide information for governors of schools maintained by LEAs and operating with fully delegated powers, the authors hope that much of the content will be of value to governors of other schools. In particular, the years since the publication of the book's second edition have seen the arrival of grant maintained (GM) schools established under the 1988 Education Reform Act.

The number of schools acquiring GM status, although small in the context of the whole educational system, has been increasing at a quickening pace. The Conservative Government has made clear its objective for all secondary schools to move to GM status, and for a number of primary schools also to follow this route.

Legal status

GM schools are a part of the maintained education system and LEAs and the DES have to pay regard to them in their planning. However, GM schools are no longer responsible to an LEA in any aspect of their work.

Acquisition of GM status

A parental ballot for GM status can be authorised in one of two ways. Either the governing body of an LEA maintained school can pass a resolution (to be confirmed at a second meeting) or parents can requisition a ballot by signing a petition. The number of signatories must be at least 20 percent of the pupil roll.

The ballot is conducted by the Electoral Reform Society and is decided by a simple majority of those parents voting. If fewer than 50 percent vote, a second ballot is held and that ballot is decisive, whatever the turnout.

If the vote is positive, the governors must publish formal proposals setting out certain details (eg admission arrangements). Objections can be made during the two month currency of the proposals. The Secretary of State for Education and Science then approves, rejects or modifies the proposals.

Responsibilities

The LEA retains certain responsibilities for pupils attending GM schools, principally:

school attendance,
home-school transport,
provision for pupils with statements of special education needs,
clothing grants,
careers service.

Otherwise, the GM school operates as an autonomous institution, subject to the Education Acts. Governors carry the full responsibilities of an employer and set key policies such as admissions to the school.

Funding

GM schools receive in grant from the DES the annual sum they would have obtained as an LEA school funded by the local formula. To compensate for services no longer received automatically from the LEA, GM schools receive a percentage addition to their basic budget. The sum (minus the cost of services which LEAs must continue to provide) is deducted from the Revenue Support Grant paid by government to the school's former LEA.

GM schools also receive from the DES annual amounts for government-funded activities like teacher support and training, provision for pupils of New Commonwealth origin and TVEI. The allocation to the LEA is reduced accordingly. The DES also makes available a one-off grant to enable the school to equip itself to operate independently of the LEA.

GM schools receive an annual grant for minor building work and can bid to the DES for capital funding of major works.

Successful bids are paid at 100 percent, whatever the school's former status.

Implications

The arrival of GM status has produced national and local controversy and has raised fundamental issues about equality of opportunity within the maintained sector. Governors find themselves very much at the centre of the debate since their lead will very often prove decisive in determining a school's future status. Each governor will reach an individual decision in the light of local circumstances and personal principles, but the crucial responsibility will be to reach that decision in consideration of all its implications for the school and pupils, present and future.

Growth in the GM sector will have a direct effect on LEAs which will suffer a corresponding reduction in levels of funding and extent of responsibility. Already, with LMS, many LEAs are beginning to place services to schools on a more contractual basis and this trend is bound to intensify as LEAs attempt to recoup funds by securing contracts from GM schools.

This third edition has opened and closed with the theme of change. A growing diversity of schools, within and outside the maintained sector, the prospect of radical reform in the structure and functions of local government and an increasing involvement of central government in the detailed management of the maintained education system are among the factors likely to necessitate a fourth edition.

Appendix A
National conditions of employment of teaching staff

1. Conditions of employment of head teachers
Overriding requirements

A head teacher shall carry out his professional duties in accordance with and subject to:

(1) the provisions of the Education Acts 1944 to 1988;
(2) any orders and regulations having effect thereunder;
(3) the articles of government of the school of which he is head teacher, to the extent to which their content is prescribed by statute;
(4) where the school is a voluntary school or a grant maintained school which was formerly a voluntary school, any trust deed applying in relation thereto;
(5) any scheme of local management approved or imposed by the Secretary of State under Section 34 of the Education Reform Act 1988(a);

and, to the extent to which they are not inconsistent with these conditions:

(a) provisions of the articles of government the content of which is not so prescribed;
(b) in the case of a school which has a delegated budget
   (i) any rules, regulations or policies laid down by the governing body under their powers as derived from any of the sources specified in sub-paragraphs (1) to (5) and (a) above; and
   (ii) any rules, regulations or policies laid down by his employers with respect to matters for which the governing body is not so responsible;
(c) in any other case, any rules, regulations or policies laid down by his employers; and
(d) the terms of his appointment.

General functions

Subject to the paragraphs above, the head teacher shall be responsible for the internal organisation, management and control of the school.

Consultation

In carrying out his duties the head teacher shall consult, where this is appropriate, with the Authority, the Governing Body, the staff of the school and the parents of its pupils.

Professional duties

The professional duties of a head teacher shall include:

School aims	(1)	formulating the overall aims and objectives of the school and policies for their implementation;
Appointment of staff	(2)	participating in the selection and appointment of the teaching and non-teaching staff of the school;

Management of staff   (3) (a) deploying and managing all teaching and non-teaching staff of the school and allocating particular duties to them (including such duties of the head teacher as may properly be delegated to the deputy head teacher or other members of the staff), in a manner consistent with their conditions of employment, maintaining a reasonable balance for each teacher between work carried out in school and work carried out elsewhere;

(b) ensuring that the duty of providing cover for absent teachers is shared equitably among all teachers in the school (including the head teacher), taking account of their teaching and other duties;

Liaison with staff unions and associations   (4) maintaining relationships with organisations representing teachers and other persons on the staff of the school;

Curriculum   (5) (a) determining, organising and implementing an appropriate curriculum for the school, having regard to the needs, experience, interests, aptitudes

and stage of development of the pupils and the resources available to the
school; and his duty under Sections 1(1)
and 10(1)(b) and (2) of the Education
Act 1988;

(b) securing that all pupils in attendance at
the school take part in daily collective
worship in pursuance of his duty under
Section 10(1)(a) of the Education Reform
Act 1988;

Review

(6) keeping under review the work and organisation of the school;

*Standards of
teaching and
learning*

(7) evaluating the standards of teaching and
learning in the school, and ensuring that
proper standards of professional performance are established and maintained;

*Appraisal, training
development of staff*

(8) (a) supervising and participating in
arrangements made in accordance with
regulations made under Section 49 of the
Education (No. 2) Act 1986(b) for the appraisal of the performance of teachers in
the school; participating in arrangements
made for the appraisal of his performance
as head teacher, and that of other head
teachers who are the responsibility of
the same appraising body in accordance
with such regulations; participating in
the identification of areas in which he
would benefit from further training and
undergoing such training;

(b) ensuring that all staff in the school have
access to advice and training appropriate to their needs, in accordance with
the policies of the maintaining authority
or, in the case of a grant maintained
school, of the governing body, for the
development of staff;

*Management
information*

(9) providing information about the work and
performance of the staff employed at the
school where this is relevant to their future
employment;

Pupil progress

(10) ensuring that the progress of the pupils of
the school is monitored and recorded;

Pastoral care

(11) determining and ensuring the implementation of a policy for the pastoral care of the pupils;

Discipline

(12) determining, in accordance with any written statement of general principles provided for him by the governing body, measures to be taken with a view to promoting, among the pupils, self-discipline and proper regard for authority, encouraging good behaviour on the part of the pupils, securing that the standard of behaviour of the pupils is acceptable and otherwise regulating the conduct of the pupils; making such measures generally known within the school, and ensuring that they are implemented.

(13) ensuring the maintenance of good order and discipline at all times during the school day (including the midday break) when pupils are present on the school premises and whenever the pupils are engaged in authorised school activities, whether on the school premises or elsewhere;

Relations with parents

(14) making arrangements for parents to be given regular information about the school curriculum, the progress of their children and other matters affecting the school, so as to promote common understanding of its aims;

Relations with other bodies

(15) promoting effective relationships with persons and bodies outside the school;

Relations with governing body

(16) advising and assisting the governing body of the school in the exercise of its functions, including (without prejudice to any rights he may have as a governor of the school), attending meetings of the governing body and making such reports to it in connection with the discharge of his functions as it may properly require either on a regular basis or from time to time;

Relations with authority

(17) (except in the case of grant maintained schools) providing for liaison and co-operation with the officers of the maintaining authority; making such reports to the authority in connection with the dis-

charge of his functions as it may properly require, either on a regular basis or from time to time;

Relations with other educational establishments

(18) maintaining liaison with other schools and further education establishments with which the school has a relationship;

Resources

(19) allocating, controlling and accounting for those financial and material resources of the school which are under the control of the head teacher;

Premises

(20) making arrangements, if so required by the maintaining authority or the governing body of a grant maintained school (as appropriate), for the security and effective supervision of the school buildings and their contents and of the school grounds; and ensuring (if so required) that any lack of maintenance is promptly reported to the maintaining authority or, if appropriate, the governing body;

Absence

(21) arranging for a deputy head teacher or other suitable person to assume responsibility for the discharge of his functions as head teacher at any time when he is absent from the school;

Teaching

(22) participating, to such extent as may be appropriate having regard to his other duties, in the teaching of pupils at the school, including the provision of cover for absent teachers.

Daily break

A head teacher shall be entitled to a break of reasonable length in the course of each school day, and shall arrange for a suitable person to assume responsibility for the discharge of his functions as head teacher during that break.

2. Conditions of employment of deputy head teachers
Professional duties

A person appointed deputy head teacher in a school, in addition to carrying out the professional duties of a school teacher,

School Governors

including those duties particularly assigned to him by the head teacher, shall:

(1) assist the head teacher in managing the school or such part of it as may be determined by the head teacher;
(2) undertake any professional duty of the head teacher which may be delegated to him by the head teacher;
(3) undertake, in the absence of the head teacher and to the extent required by him or the relevant body or, in the case of an aided school, the governing body, the professional duties of the head teacher;
(4) be entitled to a break of reasonable length in the course of each school day.

3. Conditions of employment of school teachers
Exercise of general professional duties

A teacher who is not a head teacher shall carry out the professional duties of a school teacher as circumstances may require:

(1) if he is employed as a teacher in a school, under the reasonable direction of the head teacher of that school;
(2) if he is employed by an authority on terms under which he is not assigned to any one school, under the reasonable direction of that authority and of the head teacher of any school in which he may for the time being be required to work as a teacher.

Exercise of particular duties

(1) A teacher employed as a teacher (other than a head teacher) in a school shall perform, in accordance with any directions which may reasonably be given to him by the head teacher from time to time, such particular duties as may reasonably be assigned to him.
(2) A teacher employed by an authority on terms such as those described in paragraph (2) above shall perform, in accordance with any direction which may reasonably be given to him from time to time by the authority or by the head teacher of any school in which he may for the time being be required to work as a teacher, such particular duties as may reasonably be assigned to him.

Professional duties

The following duties shall be deemed to be included in the professional duties which a school teacher may be required to perform:

Teaching

(1) (a) planning and preparing courses and lessons;

(b) teaching, according to their educational needs, the pupils assigned to him, including the setting and marking of work to be carried out by the pupil in school and elsewhere;

(c) assessing, recording and reporting on the development, progress and attainment of pupils;

in each case having regard to the curriculum for the school.

Other activities

(2) (a) promoting the general progress and well-being of individual pupils and of any class or group of pupils assigned to him;

(b) providing guidance and advice to pupils on educational and social matters and on their further education and future careers, including information about sources of more expert advice on specific questions; making relevant records and reports;

(c) making records of and reports on the personal and social needs of pupils;

(d) communicating and consulting with the parents of pupils;

(e) communicating and co-operating with persons or bodies outside the school;

(f) participating in meetings arranged for any of the purposes described above;

Assessments and reports

(3) providing or contributing to oral and written assessments, reports and references relating to individual pupils and groups of pupils;

Appraisal

(4) participating in arrangements made in accordance with regulations made under Section 49 of the Education (No. 2) Act 1986 for the appraisal of his performance and that of other teachers;

Review: further training and development

(5) (a) reviewing from time to time his methods of teaching and programmes of work.

(b) participating in arrangements for his further training and professional development as a teacher;

Educational methods

(6) advising and co-operating with the head teacher and other teachers (or any one or more of them) on the preparation and development of courses of study, teaching materials, teaching programmes, methods of teaching and assessment and pastoral arrangements;

Discipline, health and safety

(7) maintaining good order and discipline among the pupils and safeguarding their health and safety both when they are authorised to be on the school premises and when they are engaged in authorised school activities elsewhere;

Staff meetings

(8) participating in meetings at the school which relate to the curriculum for the school or the administration or organisation of the school, including pastoral arrangements;

Cover

(9) supervising and so far as practicable teaching any pupils whose teacher is not available to teach them:

provided that no teacher shall be required to provide such cover:

(a) after the teacher who is absent or otherwise not available has been so for three or more consecutive working days; or

(b) where the fact that the teacher would be absent or otherwise not available for a period exceeding three consecutive working days was known to the maintaining authority or, in the case of a grant maintained school or a school which has a delegated budget and whose local management scheme delegates the relevant responsibility for the provision of supply teachers to the governing body, to the governing body for two or more working days before the absence commenced;

unless:

(i)   he is a teacher employed wholly or mainly for the purpose of providing such cover ('a supply teacher'): or

(ii)   the authority or the governing body (as the case may be) have exhausted all reasonable means of providing a supply teacher to provide cover without success; or

(iii) he is a full-time teacher at the school but has been assigned by the head teacher in the time-table to teach or carry out other specified duties (except cover) for less than 75% of those hours in the week during which pupils are taught at the school;

Public examinations

(10) participating in arrangements for preparing pupils for public examinations and in assessing pupils for the purposes of such examinations; recording and reporting such assessments and participating in arrangements for pupils' presentation for and supervision during such examinations;

Management

(11)(a) contributing to the selection for appointment and professional development of other teachers and non-teaching staff, including the induction and assessment of new and probationary teachers;

(b) co-ordinating or managing the work of other teachers;

(c) taking such part as may be required of him in the review, development and management of activities relating to the curriculum, organisation and pastoral functions of the school;

Administration

(12)(a) participating in administrative and organisational tasks related to such duties as are described above, including the management or supervision of persons providing support for the teachers in the school and the ordering and allocation of equipment and materials;

(b) attending assemblies, registering the attendance of pupils and supervising pupils, whether these duties are to be performed before, during or after school sessions.

Working time

(1) (a)   a teacher employed full-time, other than in the circumstances described in sub-paragraph (c), shall be available for work for 195 days in any year, of which 190 days shall be days on which he may be required to teach pupils in addition to carrying out other duties; and those 195 days shall be specified by his employer or, if the employer so directs, by the head teacher;

(b)   such a teacher shall be available to perform such duties at such times and such places as may be specified by the head teacher (or, where the teacher is not assigned to any one school, by his employer or the head teacher of any school in which he may for the time being be required to work as a teacher) for 1,265 hours in any year, those hours to be allocated reasonably throughout those days in the year on which he is required to be available for work;

(c)   sub-paragraphs (a) and (b) do not apply to such a teacher employed wholly or mainly to teach or perform other duties in relation to pupils in a residential establishment;

(d)   time spent in travelling to or from the place of work shall not count against the 1,265 hours referred to in sub-paragraph (b);

(e)   such a teacher shall not be required under his contract as a teacher to undertake midday supervision, and shall be allowed a break of reasonable length either between school sessions or between the hours of 12 noon and 2.00 p.m.;

(f)   such a teacher shall, in addition to the requirements set out in sub-paragraphs (a) and (b) above, work such additional hours as may be needed to enable him to discharge effectively his professional duties, including, in particular, the marking of pupils' work, the writing of reports on pupils and the preparation of lessons, teaching material and teaching programmes. The amount of time required for this purpose beyond the 1,265 hours referred to in sub-paragraph (b) and the times outside the 1,265 specified hours at which duties shall be performed shall not be defined by the employer but shall depend upon the work needed to discharge the teacher's duties.

(2) In this paragraph, 'year' means a period of 12 months commencing on 1st September unless the school's academic year begins in August in which case it means a period of 12 months commencing on 1st August.

Appendix B
Composition of governing bodies of maintained schools

Sections 3 and 4 of the Education Act 1986 specify the basic composition of governing bodies for county, controlled and maintained special schools, and set out the numbers and categories of governor for aided and special agreement schools. Section 53 of the 1988 Education Reform Act details the constitution of grant maintained schools' governing bodies.

County, controlled and special schools

The following table details how the governing body must be comprised:

Pupil numbers	Parents	LEA	Head teacher (if he so chooses)	Teacher	Co-opted (or for controlled schools: foundation/co-opted)*	Total
Up to 99	2	2	1	1	3 (2/1)	9
100–299	3	3	1	1	4 (3/1)	12
300–599	4	4	1	2	5 (4/1)	16
600 or more	5	5	1	2	6 (4/2)	19

Table 1 Appendix B: Composition of governing body

*There are circumstances in which the number of co-opted governors will be reduced:

(a)   If a county or controlled primary school serves an area in which there is a minor authority, that authority will appoint one governor.

(b)   The District Health Authority will appoint one governor at a hospital special school.

(c)   At other special schools one (less than 100 pupils) or two (more than 99 pupils) may be appointed by appropriate voluntary organisations designated by the LEA.

Aided and special agreement schools

The exact composition of the governing body is not prescribed as for other maintained schools. The governing body must reflect the legal duty to include:

(a)   At least one LEA governor.

(b)   At least one minor authority governor if the school is a primary school serving such an area.

(c)   Foundation governors* (to include at least one parent of a pupil).

(d)   At least one parent governor.

(e)   At least one (schools with fewer than 300 pupils) or two teacher governors.

(f)   The head if he so chooses.

*The foundation governors must outnumber all other governors (always including the head) by two if the governing body is 18 or less or by three if the governing body is larger.

Grant maintained schools

The composition must provide for:

(a)   Five parent governors.

(b)   At least one but not more than two teacher governors.

(c)   The head (*ex officio*).

(d)   First governors (for ex-county schools) or foundation governors (for ex-voluntary schools). These governors must outnumber the other governors and must include at least two parents of current pupils.

The Secretary of State has power to appoint one or two additional governors. If he does so, that can be balanced by an increase in first or foundation governors.

Appendix C
Suggestions for further reading

The changes brought by the 1988 Education Reform Act have been so profound that much excellent material produced earlier has become outdated. The following selection of recent publications is by no means exhaustive. More comprehensive bibliographies will be available from LEA co-ordinators for governor training.

Advisory Centre for Education: *Governors Handbook* ACE 1988 ISBN 0 900029811 £4.50

Beckett Cynthia, Bell Les and Rhodes Chris: *Working with Governors in Schools* Open University Press ISBN 0 335094279 £10.99

Brooksbank Kenneth and Nice David: *County and Voluntary Schools* Longman 2nd edition 1989 ISBN 0 582033411 £17.50

Bullivant Barbara: *You are the Governor* Bedford Square Press 2nd edition 1989 ISBN 0 719912334 £4.50

Department of Education and Science: *School Governors: A guide to the Law*, Volume 1 — *County and Controlled Schools* and Volume 2 — *Aided and Special Agreement Schools* DES 1988 Free, distributed and updated via LEAs.

Everard Bertie and Morris Geoffrey: *Effective School Management* Paul Chapman Publishing Ltd 1990 ISBN 1 853960861 £10.95

Her Majesty's Inspectorate: *Special Needs Issues* HMSO 1990 ISBN 0 11270722x £2.95

Hume Colin: *Grievance and Discipline in Schools* Longman 1989 ISBN 0 582062551 £6.50

Hume Colin: *Effective Staff Selection in Schools* Longman 1990 ISBN 0 58206256X £6.50

Lawson Bridget: *Pupil Discipline and Exclusion in Schools* Longman/AGIT 1991 ISBN 0 582083842 £6.95

Leonard Martin: *The School Governors' Handbook* Oxford, Blackwell Education ISBN 0 631170650 £6.95

Lowe Chris: *The School Governor's Legal Guide* Croner Publications 2nd edition 1989 ISBN 1 854520318

Lowe Chris: *Insurance and Law for Schools* Hobsons Publishing 1991 £4.50

Newell Peter: *ACE Special Education Handbook — The Law on Children with Special Needs* Advisory Centre for Education 3rd edition 1989 ISBN 0 900029803

Sallis Joan: *Schools, Parents and Governors: A New Approach to Accountability* Routledge 1988 ISBN 0 415005914 £9.95

Sallis Joan: *School Governors: Your Questions Answered* Times Educational Supplement/Hodder and Stoughton 1991 ISBN 0 340547871 £6.99

Sharp Paul and Dunford John: *The Education System in England and Wales* Longman 1990 ISBN 0 582009669 £5.95

Stock Barry: *Health and Safety in Schools* Croner Publications 1991 ISBN 1 855248432 £9.95

Wallis Elizabeth: *Education A to Z: Sources on all Major Educational Topics* Advisory Centre for Education £7.95

Wragg Ted and Partington J.A.: *A Handbook for School Governors* Routledge 2nd edition 1989 ISBN 0 415038049

Journals and papers:

ACE Bulletin (bi-monthly) — from Advisory Centre for Education, 1B Aberdeen Studios, 22-24 Highbury Grove, London, N5 2EA

Education (weekly) — from Longman, Fourth Avenue, Harlow, Essex, CM19 5AA

Governors' Action (bi-monthly) — from AGIT, c/o CEDC, Lyng Hall, Blackberry Lane, Coventry, CV2 3JS

Managing Schools Today (bi-monthly) — from Questions Publishing Co Ltd, 6/7 Hockley Hill, Birmingham, B18 5AA

Times Educational Supplement (weekly) — widely available

Excellent resources materials for governors are prepared by:

Action for Governors Information and Training (AGIT), c/o CEDC, Lyng Hall, Blackberry Lane, Coventry CV2 3JS

Advisory Centre for Education, 1B Aberdeen Studios, 22-24 Highbury Grove, London N5 2EA

ISCG (an independent institution for school and college governors), 194 Freston Road, London W10 6TT

National Association of Governors and Managers, Suite 36/38, 21 Bennetts Hill, Birmingham B2 5QP

Appendix D
Glossary of common terms

In such a comprehensive service as education, and one so prone to acronyms, governors are bound to meet some terms unfamiliar to them. The following list is intended to provide a helpful guide but can make no claim to completeness or legal precision.

Admission arrangements   The arrangements made by an LEA or, in the case of a voluntary aided school, the governors in consultation with the LEA, for the admission of pupils. The 1986 Education Act provides that governors must be consulted annually over the admission arrangements to the school.

Agreed syllabus   The syllabus required by the Education Act 1944 to be adopted by an LEA for religious education in county and controlled schools, to be drawn up and reviewed by a Standing Advisory Council on Religious Education (q.v.).

Aided school   A type of voluntary school which is not provided by the LEA, though the LEA bears the greater part of the running costs of the school. The premises of an aided school are owned by trustees and the governors have distinctive powers as detailed in the articles of government for the school. The governors of aided schools are the employers of the teachers and control the admission of pupils.

Appeals procedures   LEA and voluntary aided governor decisions over pupil admissions can be referred by parents to Appeals Committees set up under the 1980 Education Act. LEA decisions relating to special educational needs can be appealed under the 1981 Education Act. A formal appeal procedure over pupil exclusions was established by the 1986 Education Act.

Articles of government   The document which describes the powers and duties of the governing body. All governors must be given a copy of the articles of government for their school.

Attendance statistics   From the summer 1992 all schools are required to publish annual statistics relating to pupil attendance.

Audit Commission   The agency established by government to monitor the use of funds by local authorities and to promote good practice and efficient working in local government. (See also District Audit.)

Capital expenditure The spending on large-scale building projects, such as the provision and extension of schools. Purchase of some major items of equipment may also count as capital expenditure. Levels of capital expenditure by LEAs are controlled by central government as a part of its public expenditure policies. Capital expenditure is normally funded through loans.

Careers service The service provided by an LEA to help young people in their choice of careers, further education and training. In addition to the careers education programmes provided in schools by teachers, careers officers will visit in order to provide information and advice to senior pupils.

Chief education officer (CEO) Also known in some LEAs as director of education, director of educational services, education officer or education secretary. It is a statutory requirement for an LEA to appoint a chief officer whose function is to advise the LEA and to implement its policies.

Child Guidance Service A service to help children and families experiencing behavioural and emotional difficulties. Among the professions brought together by the service are educational psychologists, child psychiatrists and social workers.

City technology colleges (CTCs) A type of independent (but non fee-paying) secondary school established by the 1988 Education Reform Act. CTCs are managed by sponsors and are provided by a mixture of private and government funding. They are sited in urban areas and offer a curriculum with emphasis on science and technology. City Colleges for the Technology of the Arts (CCTAs) specialise in the creative and performing arts.

Clerk to the governors In effect the secretary to the governing body, responsible for drawing up agendas, advising the governors on matters of procedure and actioning governors' decisions. After consulting with the CEO, governors select their own clerk who is then appointed by the LEA.

Commission for Racial Equality The agency established under the Race Relations Act to monitor and report on discrimination against minority ethnic groups in Great Britain. The Commission has powers to investigate allegations of discrimination and to initiate Court proceedings where appropriate.

Compulsory school age A child attains compulsory school age at the beginning of the term following his fifth birthday. He ceases to be of compulsory school age in the year in which he becomes 16. Those children with sixteenth birthdays falling between 1st September and 31st January may leave school at the end of the Easter term, and those with birthdays between 1st

February and 31st August may leave on the Friday before the last Monday in May (i.e. the summer half term holiday).

Controlled school A type of voluntary school which is not provided by an LEA although the LEA maintains the school and is the employer of the teachers. The ownership of the premises is vested in trustees.

County school A school established, owned and maintained by an LEA

Department of Education and Science (DES) The government department responsible for the education service under its political head, the Secretary of State for Education and Science. Primary and secondary education in Wales is the responsibility of the Welsh Office under the Secretary of State for Wales.

Destination statistics From summer 1992 all secondary schools are required to publish details of the routes (employment, training, further/higher education, etc.) taken by those leaving the school.

District auditor An official appointed by the Audit Commission, responsible for monitoring the financial performance of local government in a specific area of the country.

Education Assets Board The agency established by the 1988 Education Reform Act to oversee the transfer of assets from LEAs to the governors of grant maintained schools (q.v.).

Education committee The committee set up by an LEA, with delegated responsibility for the provision of education in the authority's area. The majority of the education committee will be elected councillors, together with teacher and church representatives.

Equal Opportunities Commission The body established under the Sex Discrimination Act 1975 to monitor the effect of equal opportunities legislation and to investigate individual complaints of discrimination on the grounds of gender. The EOC may take cases to court under the equal opportunities legislation.

Examination statistics Secondary schools are required to publish detailed results of public examinations in the school prospectus (q.v.). From summer 1992 LEAs are required to publish summary results for the schools in their area.

Family centres A type of provision for pre-school children and their families offering a range of activities. The Children Act 1989 establishes family centres to serve a wider age group of children in need.

First school A school with an age range from 4-5 to 8 or 9 years old.

Form entry (f.e.) This is a convenient way of describing the size of a school by reference to the number of classes in each year group. A form of entry is usually regarded as 30 pupils, so that a comprehensive school admitting annually 240 pupils would be described as an 8 form entry (or 8 f.e.) school.

Four term year An alternative way of organising the school year to provide four terms of almost equal length. There is growing interest at local and national level in the possible adoption of a four term year in this country.

Further education Part-time or full-time education normally provided in or by colleges of further education for people over the statutory school leaving age.

Grants for Education and Support Training (GEST) A system of central government grants supported by local funds through which government promotes specific educational developments. The former Education Support Grants (ESG) and LEA Training Grants Scheme (LEATGS) are now subsumed within GEST.

Governors' organisations There are a number of national organisations established to promote the interests and develop the expertise of governors. Details will be found in Appendix C.

Grant maintained schools A type of school established under the 1988 Education Act which receives its funding direct from government which subtracts the funding from the Revenue Support Grant (q.v.) paid to local authorities. Grant maintained schools also receive additional sums to compensate them for the loss of central services and GEST funding.

Group sizes The system laid down under the Pay and Conditions Document which establishes minimum and maximum payments for head teachers and deputy head teachers according to the number and age of pupils at the school. There are six different group sizes of school.

Her Majesty's Inspectorate (HMI) HMI are appointed by the Queen in Council to inspect and report to the Secretary of State for Education and Science on the standard of education provided in the country's schools.

Higher education This general term describes national institutions such as universities, polytechnics and colleges of higher education.

Incentive allowances These are the additional payments which governors can make to teachers who carry extra responsibility or who demonstrate outstanding ability. There are five allowances, A–E.

Independent schools These schools do not receive direct government funding (except CTCs). They are subject to inspection by HMI but are not required to provide the National Curriculum.

Infant school A type of school which provides education for children aged 4/5 to 7 years old.

Instrument of government The instrument of government sets out the composition of the governing body and its rules for the conduct of meetings. All governors are to receive a copy of the instrument of government for their school.

Junior school This is a school which provides education for children between the ages of 7 and 11.

Local education authority (LEA) The council of a shire country, metropolitan district or London borough. In practice, the LEA will usually delegate the greater part of its educational responsibility to its Education Committee.

Maintained school A school which is maintained at public expense. The term describes LEA, voluntary and grant maintained schools.

Middle school A school normally providing a four year course for pupils aged 8–12 or 9–13.

Minor authority In an English shire county a minor authority can be either a district council or parish council; in a Welsh County, a district council or community council. Minor authorities have rights of representation on the governing body of LEA maintained primary schools.

Minor works This is capital building work costing less than £200,000 (county and controlled schools) or £250,000 (aided schools) and counting against the LEA's capital allocation from the DES.

More open enrolment This is the term used for the clauses in the 1988 Education Reform Act which provide that primary and secondary schools shall admit pupils to their physical capacity if there is such demand.

National Curriculum Council (England) and the Curriculum Council for Wales The bodies established under the 1988 Education Reform Act to advise the Secretaries of State on the curriculum and to publish information relating to the school curriculum.

National Vocational Qualifications (NVQs) These comprise a national system for accrediting standards in vocational work. They are validated by a National Council for Vocational Qualifications.

Nursery education This describes pre-school education for children from the age of 2. LEA's have a power, but not a duty, to provide nursery education which can be delivered either through separate schools or through nursery units attached to infant or primary schools.

Parent – Teacher Association Many schools have developed such associations in order to promote partnership between parents and teachers and to engage in educational, social and fund-raising activities.

Pre-School Playgroups These provide part-time day care for pre-school children and are run by volunteer parents. Most playgroups are affiliated to the Pre-School Playgroups Association.

Primary School This is a school which combines both infant and junior education. It is also sometimes known as a JMI school — i.e. junior mixed and infant.

Probationary Teacher The term which used to be applied to newly–qualified teachers during their first year of service when it was probationary.

Prospectus All schools are required to publish annually information about themselves to current and prospective parents. The minimum requirements for the school prospectus are to be found in the articles of government.

Pupil-Teacher Ratio A method of expressing the teacher staffing resources within a school. A school of 200 and a staff (including the head) of 10 would have a pupil-teacher ratio of 20.0. Before formula–funding most LEAs used to set schools' staffing by reference to pupil–teacher ratios.

Qualified Teacher Status (QTS) A qualified teacher is one who has satisfied the requirements of the Secretary of State and consequently been accorded Qualified Teacher Status.

Reception class The class in the infant, first or primary school to which young children are admitted on first entry at or before the age of five.

Reserved teacher A teacher appointed to a voluntary controlled or special agreement school to give Religious Education in accordance with the denomination of the school.

Revenue expenditure In contrast to capital expenditure, revenue expenditure is annually recurrent and is used to pay for the running of the school.

Revenue support grant This is the money which central government provides to local authorities for the provision of services. The allocation is made according to a complex formula which attempts to quantify local needs.

Rising fives A term used to describe children who are admitted to the reception class at the beginning of the term in which they will become five.

School attendance order If parents fail to arrange for children to receive efficient and suitable full-time education, the LEA has power to issue a school attendance order requiring the parent to cause the child to attend a school named in the order.

School Examinations and Assessment Council (SEAC) The national body responsible for advising the Secretary of State on examinations and assessment and responsible for publishing information to schools and others.

School hours There are no minimum hours set down in law, but the DES has advised that the National Curriculum is unlikely to be provided satisfactorily unless the following minimum weekly lesson times are provided:

Age	Hours
5–7	21
8–11	23.5
12–16	24 (possibly 25 for 14–16 year olds)

School Teachers Review Body This is the standing review body which advises the Secretary of State on teachers' pay and conditions.

Secondary school A school providing for children aged 11 and over. In LEAs which have first and middle schools, pupils may start secondary schooling at the age of 12 or 13. Secondary schools may or may not provide sixth form education.

Secretary of State for Education and Science The political head of the Department of Education and Science, who is a member of the Cabinet.

Secretary of State for Wales The Minister who, under the Education Acts, exercises responsibility for schools in Wales. The Secretary of State for Education and Science retains responsibility for teachers in both England and Wales.

Section . . . Some important measures are described by reference to the law which enacted them:

Section 11 (of the 1966 Local Government Act): A system of Home Office funding providing 75% support to approved programmes of educational support for members of minority ethnic communities.

Section 12 and 13 (of the 1980 Education Act): The procedures which LEAs and voluntary aided governors must follow when proposing the opening, closure or reorganisation of schools.

Sections 42 and 50 (of the 1988 Education Reform Act): Both provisions require LEAs to draw up and publish to governors detailed statements of the intended and actual budget share allocated to schools. Section 42 refers to schools operating under full LMS and Section 50 to other maintained schools.

Sixth form college An institution providing education for pupils aged 16–19 and which is administered legally as a school.

Special agreement school A small category of voluntary schools similar in many respects to voluntary aided schools and differing mainly in the historical circumstances of their establishment.

Special class/unit Specialist provision for children with SEN is often provided in a class or unit attached to a mainstream school.

Special educational needs (SEN) The 1981 Education Act established the concept of special educational needs as a basis on which special, or separate, arrangements may need to be made for the education of certain pupils. These are described as pupils having a significantly greater degree of difficulty in learning than the majority of pupils of their age.

Special school A school providing educational facilities for children with serious or complex long-term educational needs.

Standard Attainment Tasks (SATs) These are the test measures by which attainment in the National Curriculum is evaluated.

Standard number This represents the minimum number of pupils which a primary or secondary school must admit according to demand. The standard number must be subject to regular review.

Standard Spending Assessment (SSA) This is the central government assumption of the spending levels which local authorities need to provide for their different services.

Standing Advisory Council on Religious Education (SACRE) The body which advises the LEA on religious worship in county schools and Religious Education provided in accordance within an agreed syllabus. The SACRE is made up of four committees representing the LEA, the teachers' associations, the Church of England and other Christian and principal religious traditions in the area.

Supply teacher A teacher employed to fill a temporary vacancy in the staff of a school, usually on a day to day basis.

Support staff This is the generic term used to describe the school staff who are not teachers.

Teachers' associations The six associations recognised nationally are: the Assistant Masters and Mistresses Association (AMMA), the National Association of Head Teachers (NAHT), the National Union of Teachers (NUT), the National Association of Schoolmasters/Union of Women Teachers (NAS/UWT), the Professional Association of Teachers (PAT) and the Secondary Heads Association (SHA).

Technical and Vocational Education Initiative (and Extension) (TVEI/TVEE) A government-funded programme to boost technical and vocational education for 14–18 year olds in schools and colleges.

Tertiary college A college which brings together in one institution sixth form and non-advanced further education and is administered under the regulations for colleges of further education.

Training credits The government scheme under which school leavers are credited with funds which they can choose to spend on specific training.

Trust deed In a voluntary school the trust deed is the legal document relating to the establishment of the school and specifying the purposes and principles which must govern the conduct of the school.

Virement The process under which sums can be transferred from one budget head to another.

Voluntary schools The generic term used for schools which are not provided by the LEA, although the LEA bears the greater part of the running costs of the school. The three types of voluntary school are aided, controlled and special agreement schools.

Walking distance This is the distance as defined in the 1944 Educational Act beyond which LEAs are required to become responsible for children's transport to and from school. For children under 8 the distance (by the nearest available route) must not exceed two miles and for children over 8, three miles. LEAs have power to provide transport for children living within walking distance and are required to consider the age of the pupil and the nature of the route which he could reasonably be expected to take to and from school.

Year group A standard method of describing the stage of a child's educational career between 5 and 18. It runs from R (Reception). Years 1 and 2 (Infant), Years 3–6 (Junior), Years 7–11 (Secondary) to Years 12–13 (Sixth form). It is generally abbreviated to Y6 etc.

Youth Service Through their statutory youth service (often supplemented by grants to voluntary organisations) LEAs provide cultural and recreational opportunities for young people outside of school hours.

Youth Training Scheme (YTS) A national scheme providing full-time work experience and vocational training for young people after leaving school.

Index